Theory of
Psychoanalytic
Therapy

Other Books By Benjamin Wolstein

FREEDOM TO EXPERIENCE

IRRATIONAL DESPAIR

COUNTERTRANSFERENCE

TRANSFERENCE

EXPERIENCE AND VALUATION

THEORY OF PSYCHOANALYTIC THERAPY

BENJAMIN WOLSTEIN, Ph.D.

*Faculty, W. A. White Institute of Psychiatry,
Psychoanalysis and Psychology; Clinical Professor
of Psychology, Adelphi University*

GRUNE & STRATTON   NEW YORK • LONDON

Library of Congress Catalog Card No. 67-11953

Printed in U.S.A. (G-B)

Contents

Illustrations

FIGURES

TABLES

Preface

This study further explores recent formulations of psycho-analytic therapy.[1]* The practicing psychoanalyst will find it worthwhile, of course, to consult them as background and perspective of the present study. But he may also consider it separately. For it is an independent attempt to treat psychoanalysis as neither a tributary of general and experimental psychology nor a grid for any one metapsychology but, primarily, as an empirical, systematic and interpretive structure of therapeutic inquiry. No matter how it is related to neurology, physiology or medicine, to psychology, sociology or economics, to morals, religion or philosophy, these relations fail to meet the issues head on—first, to demarcate a structure of inquiry which many different psychoanalysts use with many different patients and, second, to make interpretive and speculative room for all co-participants to experience the psychoanalytic work in ways which are directly suited to their individual personalities. At the foundations, then, are no contradictions or inconsistencies between a unified structure of inquiry and a plurality of therapeutic experiences. To those absurdist and mystical doctrines, moreover, which are still rooted in the culture at large and in some quarters of psychology and psychotherapy, the most powerful answer is obviously that which embodies and, therefore, yields true psychoanalytic knowledge— a well ordered structure of inquiry. The following study is a contribution to this answer.

In the first chapter, the experience of psychoanalytic therapy

* For Notes to the Preface, see page 204.

is reviewed from empirical, systematic and interpretive points of view. In the second, a structure of psychoanalytic inquiry is sketched and illustrated while, in the third, its five orders are explored in greater detail. Symbolic operations are developed in the fourth, representing transference as t_n, resistance as r_n, anxiety as a_n and counteranxiety as ca_n, counterresistance as cr_n, countertransference as ct_n in the first order of observation; transference as t, resistance as r, anxiety as a and counteranxiety as ca, counterresistance as cr, countertransference as ct in the second order of definition; genesis as G, function as F, structure as S, dynamism as D, immediacy as I and reflection as R in the third order of postulation; theory of unconscious experience as U in the fourth order of explanation; and metapsychologies as $[M_n]$ in the fifth order of interpretation. This structure of inquiry and its symbolic representation are set forth on an experimental basis, to be enlarged for future requirements and modified by the collaborative efforts of others. But since they are still experimental, the twenty symbols are identified, here, for easy reference. See Table 1, as well, for an outline of this notational scheme.[2] The last chapter describes, briefly, how this structure may be applied to a most significant distinction for all perspectives on psychoanalytic inquiry, that of awareness and responsibility.

Again, I thank Jules Altman for indexing this work and for his comments about various drafts of its development. I am indebted to my colleagues at the Sixth International Congress for Psychotherapy for the invitation to read "The Unity of Psychoanalytic Therapy" in August, 1964, which I rewrite as Chapter 1, B; in the Postdoctoral Program for Psychotherapy at Adelphi University for scheduling "A Notational Scheme for Psychoanalytic Inquiry" at its Workshop in Psychotherapy in March, 1965, and on the editorial board of *Selected Papers on Psychotherapy* (Garden City: Adelphi University, 1965) for publishing it as "Notes on Psychoanalytic Structure," which I revise as Chapter 2, A; in the Professional Association of the Postgraduate Center for Mental Health for the opportunity to present "Further Reflections on Countertransference" in January, 1966, which I adapt as Chapter 1, A, (1); and in the Association for the Advancement of Psychoanalysis for the invitation to a panel discussion of "Determinism and Freedom" in May, 1966, from which I reorganize my comments as Chapter 5. But I am grateful, above all, to my friends and students at Adelphi University, New School for Social Research and W. A. White Institute of Psychiatry, Psychoanalysis and Psychology, who first heard these ideas in the making. I thank them, now, with affection and esteem.

—B. W.

Westhampton Beach
August, 1966

Theory of Psychoanalytic Therapy

Chapter 1

Experience of Therapy

SIMPLY TO RAISE the question, "How does the psycho-analyst use his experience?" indicates the vast changes in theory and practice which have taken place during the last decade. It openly and directly acknowledges that every psychoanalyst uses personal experience and, moreover, that he always puts a personal stamp on his therapeutic efforts with every patient. Chosen at random or paired by design, no two psychoanalysts with any one patient and no two patients with any one psychoanalyst are now expected to obtain exactly the same result in exactly the same way. As a practical and unquestioned postulate, it is now assumed that all persons in psychoanalysis—meaning to include, by this, all psychoanalysts and all their patients—extend individual responses to their co-participants and receive individual responses from them. Review any list of personal qualities attributed to human beings in general, and it no doubt provides a fair range of the qualities which may be attributed to psychoanalysts as well. Neither psychoanalyst nor patient, however, can tell his co-participant what he should believe the other's personal qualities are, and how he should believe they affect the other's participation in therapy. This is so because the psychoanalyst, for example, may unconsciously portray a self-image to have his patient see him as being one thing in the experiential field of therapy when he is in fact another, or because he may unconsciously direct his patient's attention along one continuum of personal qualities when his patient could more profitably direct his attention elsewhere. But

1

since the patient eventually has to make up his own mind about his psychoanalyst's personal qualities, before or after the end of therapy, efforts at portraying self-images are actually superfluous.

Is this, then, the way it really is? Are the uses of personal experience in psychoanalytic therapy so basically individual, so radically empirical, so very difficult to blueprint? If a psychoanalyst does not happen to think they are, perhaps he also has not yet come to terms with the therapeutic effects of his multidimensional self—which need not necessarily be negative so long as his patient has not yet come to terms with the therapeutic effects of his either. But if a patient begins to develop deeper awareness of himself and, as one result, begins to develop deeper awareness of his psychoanalyst, it would be rather incongruous for the psychoanalyst to insist, in turn, on remaining unaware of how he experiences himself with that particular patient. Hard and disillusioning though the fact may appear, he has no claim to special status as one who can simply erase his operant being from the awareness of others. But if this is the way it is, then the psychoanalyst had best be open to learning with and from each particular patient how he, the psychoanalyst, uses his experience with that patient. For this purpose, it is necessary to construct a model of therapy which makes room and accounts both for the psychoanalyst's use of his experience and for the patient's active collaboration in their study of it. A model of shared experience, it is proposed, supplements the model of id therapy and the model of ego or interpersonal therapy, to bring the whole range of personal psychology within the scope of psychoanalysis.[1]*

By now, of course, everyone has heard the anxious and defensive questions which are consistently raised about collaborative study of the psychoanalytic experience. Why doesn't the patient bill his psychoanalyst for collaborating in the anal-

---

* For Notes to this Chapter, see pages 204-205.

ysis of counteranxiety, counterresistance, countertransference, instead of paying fees for these phases of the work? And why doesn't the psychoanalyst also satisfy both his and his patient's libidinal impulses, when these are present, and encourage their having sexual intercourse as part of the treatment?—it is usually a male psychoanalyst asking about intercourse with an adult female, rarely with an adult male, never with a child, male or female. Since these questions most frequently are about sex and money, and least frequently about aggression, it is possible to treat them as representing the special attitudes of classical metapsychology and requiring the special procedures of id therapy. Those who do not follow the classical perspective to the end, however, need not adopt these attitudes and procedures as the overall structure of psychoanalysis. Below, these questions of sex and money are considered in other perspectives.

If it is true, now, that psychoanalyst and patient share a common field of therapeutic inquiry, it becomes necessary to enlarge the structure of psychoanalysis. It also becomes necessary to disentangle their believed metapsychologies from both the empirical observations and definitions and the systematic postulates and theory which institute this field of psychological inquiry and, then, to distinguish psychoanalysis from other psychotherapies and systematic psychologies. The critical distinction is between structure of inquiry, on the one hand, which all psychoanalysts try to realize in common, and experience of therapy, on the other, which represents a uniquely personal and interpersonal convergence of two human beings seeking psychoanalytic experience and believing metapsychologies so diverse as to stretch from the instinctual dialectics of Freudism to the Christian love of daseinanalysis.

A. SCIENCE AND ART

Consider, further, this distinction of structure of inquiry from experience of therapy, because its clear outline provides

a firm base for relating theory to practice. To this end, psychoanalysis is conceived as ordered inquiry into the experience of
relatedness and communication whose structure is made up of
observations, definitions, postulates, theory and metapsychologies. The problem, here, is to draw across this ordered structure the line which reflects both logical and clinical differences
between inquiry and therapy. In this context, recall the relation of science and art in general—science a body of observation
and definition, postulate and theory which reflects the organization of discovery and knowledge within a specific subject
matter; art the unification in actual practice of knowledge and
its subject matter. A psychoanalytic experience, from this point
of view, is a particular and concrete union of science and art
or, in terms more familiar, inquiry and therapy. As science,
the knowledge of psychoanalysis lends itself to extended scru-
tiny and reconstruction; as art, the practice of psychoanalysis
lends itself to empathic appreciation and criticism. It is not yet
possible, however, to provide full scientific explanation of
psychoanalytic experiences because these, roughly speaking, are
no more the concerns of scientific truth than are the products
of such other arts as painting or writing. A product of any art
may feel right and good, yield insight and catharsis and, in the
end, even give way to an ineffable sense of oneness. But no
work of art—whether it is a novel, a painting or a therapy—can
ever be entirely structured to result from organized and patterned inquiry. All experiences of psychoanalytic therapy,
therefore, are particular and concrete in each case, while their
structure of inquiry may be organized and patterned for all
cases.

Any description of psychoanalytic art is, in some sense, a
second-hand revival or reproduction of the original therapeutic
inquiry. Any research study of these descriptions is once again
removed, it would follow, from that original therapeutic in-

quiry. Only where both participants are kept in full ignorance of their being observed, and in no other way, is it possible even to consider studying the practice of this art at first hand. But once this is adopted as common procedure, however, and it becomes general knowledge that private communications are no longer privileged and confidential, psychoanalysis ceases to be the science and art it now is, and is capable of becoming. In this eventuality, it dies a sudden and perhaps unlamented death—which is why, incidentally, it cannot be practiced in a truly totalitarian society. On the other hand, natural obstacles to making first-hand studies from outside the experiential field of therapy may account for some special characteristics of psychoanalysis as science. It was possible, for example, to support the entire classical edifice of psychology and metapsychology with the results of but five intensive case studies and, since that pioneering work, it remains possible to contribute to the evolving structure of psychoanalysis without the support of full case studies. These natural conditions are very real; they are not easily modified or countered, to say nothing of being mastered and overcome. Recall, here, the limited utility and meager results of many mechanical devices which are being applied to the research of psychoanalytic experience; and then consider, next, certain aspects of the supervision of psychoanalytic practice.

First, the one-way vision screens, tape recordings and movies which may be useful as teaching aids in special situations but, at present, not very much more. They cannot enter into open and direct communication with the psychoanalyst's preconscious and unconscious experience from which his clinical perceptions arise, and of which he makes significant clinical judgments. No mechanical device, so far known, can enter into open and direct communication with his psychological processes and patterns in which hunches, clues, observations, definitions and their structured transformations all fall together into an integrative hypothesis concerning unconscious aspects of distortion, disturbance or difficulty—a hypothesis about which he is confident enough, finally, to offer it to his patient. Nor can such devices, so far known, enter psychological processes and patterns by which the patient works over the hypothesis—questioning, modifying, rejecting, amending, evading, enlarging, denying, affirming, accepting, assimilating—and in the end, works it through one way or another. To derive valid results, it is clear, a chemist or physicist need do no more than respect the objective conditions of his experimental work because changes in personality have no direct effects on the experimental methods which establish reliable knowledge about material entities. On the other hand, a psychoanalyst deep in the practice of his art cannot erase the effects of his personal psychology from the experiential field of his therapeutic work. Even if he could, moreover, he would not do it for the reason that, along with the effects of his personal psychology, he erases the effectiveness of his inquiry and therapy as well. Only in a most general sense, therefore, can psychoanalytic inquiry be fitted to the experimental forms of laboratory science, a sense so generalized that it does not directly contribute to our understanding of theory or practice. There is nothing in the ongoing practice of this art, furthermore, which strictly follows the experimental patterns of physics or chemistry. Neither in the derivation nor in the establishment of reliable knowledge, then, does a psychoanalyst use procedures and devices of laboratory science. Rather, he attempts to set the structure of psychoanalytic inquiry on foundations which are empirical enough to encompass great varieties of actual therapeutic experience and systematic enough to underline their distinctively psychoanalytic features.

Recall, now, certain aspects of supervision. Anyone who

supervises therapeutic work is reminded, time and again, that it is not possible to research the practice of this art at first hand. No report of clinical experience is or, indeed, contains the actual experience which is being reported. Not even through the indirect means of re-transference[2] can clinical reporting ever be or become the original experience reported. This point may appear obvious, but it is again being made to suggest the trouble with most transcendental therapies: that they would break the time barrier and have a patient live something in the therapeutic field as though he were living it entirely and absolutely for the first time; hence, their irrational despair over making this impossible ahistorical leap. At some point, every therapist has probably struggled to convey the essentials of his work with a patient, only to re-transfer into the supervisory experience his patient's distortions as distinct, clearly, from countertransferring his own. This has been observed by many different supervisors who do not at all agree on metapsychology, and it probably is best understood as the student therapist's attempt to compensate for natural and inevitable difficulties with presenting his work as he actually does it in the first instance. In no way, indeed, can he presume to revive or recount any of it so as to re-create or reproduce its original and pure form. To erase actual conditions of either the present in which any past is being relived or the experience which intervenes between past and present, then, is not only incomprehensible. To reverse time's flow is, in fact, impossible.

It is probably beyond controversy that a psychoanalyst's use of his experience begins in the art of his practice and ends in the structure of his inquiry. In daily practice with various patients, he learns to value a simple respect for his personal idiosyncracies and, as he grows, also learns to expect the open appearance of their effects in his various fields of shared experience. This fact of his scientific life is unavoidable: He cannot seek valid results while assuming that his personality and metapsychology do not at all influence his patient; nor, on the contrary, can he assume that all he does to influence his patient derives from the power of his personality and metapsychology. No psychoanalyst can expect to work well or comfortably, then, until he is both well and comfortably acquainted with his personal psychology and with turning points of his transactions where he hardens, melts, fades away. As he gets to know and accept himself in and through the changing phases of his therapeutic work, he may appropriately do anything within his range of feeling, thinking, relating—up to and including, even, the experience of his own fears and fantasies—without disrupting the psychoanalytic character of his inquiry.

(1) *Therapy*

When a psychoanalyst's response moves from the therapeutic field of experience, however, into the social field of behavior, though as social response it remains a symptom of transference, resistance, anxiety and counteranxiety, counterresistance, countertransference, he no longer can easily transform that symptom into its unconscious processes and patterns by psychological means alone. Social behavior, in fact, introduces immediate obstacles to the maintenance of psychoanalytic inquiry. Any response which makes therapeutic inquiry an ordinary social relationship, to satisfy personal needs other than those of psychoanalytic competence, usually introduces such obstacles. If, for example, a psychoanalyst literally accepts his or his patient's sexual impulses and then proceeds to enact them, he breaks out of their experiential field and into a behavioral event from which no direct return to psychotherapy is possible. Behavior institutes social actuality and, for both theory and practice, terminates psychological inquiry in depth. While its co-participants may now, of course, undertake social and moral analysis to study the meaning of this new actuality, the original field of experience is beyond direct psychological inquiry. This, most likely, is the intent of the classical suggestion to conduct therapeutic analysis of psychological processes and patterns in statu nascendi.[3] A psychoanalyst who actively seeks social relatedness with his patient—who needs him to be more than a patient, that is, in his own life—may prolong psychoanalytic inquiry far beyond its natural, useful and therapeutic terminus. The work may drag on but, whatever else it may be, it is no longer an interpersonal alliance for therapeutic purposes; it is no longer a productive working relationship. It still is relatedness and communication, of course, but it no longer is an experiential field of therapy. For all practical purposes, then, therapeutic inquiry draws to a close when a psychoanalyst generally relates to his patient as other than a troubled person striving to understand the unconscious sources of his daily distortions, disturbances and difficulties.

How far, then, can any particular psychoanalyst extend himself in behavior without disrupting the psychoanalytic character of his work? This question is neither theoretical nor scientific but, primarily, individual and practical. In daily practice, every psychoanalyst answers it in himself. Some, for example, are disturbed about meeting patients outside the consulting room in ordinary social situations—most during special phases of treatment, a few during all phases—and if they cannot face it in personal therapy, supervision, or direct exchange with the patients involved, they had better not meet them socially. A few go out of their way to do it, however, because they perceive as narrow and constricted the limits of psychoanalytic inquiry; and if they obtain useful information yet, at the same time, do not disrupt the psychological character of therapeutic inquiry, there is no a priori reason to exclude their activity from the practice of psychoanalysis. But most do not seem to mind meeting patients, accepting it as sometimes simply unavoidable in an all-too human enterprise from which the elements of chance and accident can never be entirely eliminated.

It is rumored, however, that psychoanalysts also construct and cultivate fields of therapy in which they not only enjoy elaborate fantasies with particular patients but in which, as standard operating procedure, they even have sexual intercourse as part of the session. Perhaps with the spread of this rumor to a suffering and frustrated public, patients may one day begin to request consultation, and then expect to have sexual relations as the method of treatment. Those Freudo-Darwinians who ordinarily relate in this way, it may be speculated, also probably do therapy in this way—but their activity is not, however, at all psychotherapeutic. Wishes and fantasies in the therapeutic field may be studied as containing serious problems about both identity and intimacy, instead, and about a whole range of adolescent experience whose unspeakable chaos and terror still remain to be penetrated and openly understood. No great progress has yet been made toward the resolution of these emotionally devastating problems. Consider how little attention is paid in either the culture at large or the psychoanalytic literature in particular to the pained and alienated loneliness of adolescent experience, and compare it with how much is paid to the distracting symptoms of drug addiction and drag racing, rock and roll, sexual promiscuity and confusion, hipsterism, clothes and hair styles, camp and other bits and pieces. Has the so-called identity crisis of adolescence now become so prolonged and pronounced, perhaps, because the notion of maturity remains so hard to define and rare to achieve? Does the rebellious strain of adolescence—of not being able to stay with it and, of course, not being able to leave it— result in large measure from the conflict over what to do about identity itself, once its realization is finally sighted as possible?

And psychoanalysts, it is clear, are not exempted from these social, cultural and psychological pressures on the experience of maturity. Were it not, indeed, a sad and sorry picture, it could be thought quite amusing: Imagine the psychoanalyst, especially a classical libido theorist, centering psychological therapy on the repressed aspects of his patient's infantile sexuality as though that were the main instrument of cure and then intercoursing with the patient's actual and unresolved problems of adolescent sex—yet remaining unaware, all along, that these problems are being enacted in relation to very similar ones in himself.

From a psychological point of view, the reason why sexual intercourse between psychoanalyst and patient has negative therapeutic effects is clear. A sexual wish or fantasy is, obviously, just like any other type of wish or fantasy: once fulfilled or actualized as behavior, its personal motivations need not be explored, its interpersonal meanings need not be analyzed. On the other side, the logic most probably is that after fulfilling the wish and actualizing the fantasy, both psychoanalyst and patient produce data for further exploration and analysis. To which the plain answer is, fulfillment of the unconscious wish and actualization of the conscious fantasy may become far more interesting to one or both participants than exploration of unconscious motives and analysis of conscious intentions. As a practical measure, therefore, this turn of events requires referral of both the psychoanalyst and the patient to obtain further personal therapy. For it is conceivable, despite the scarcity of clear reports about its actually happening, that a practicing psychoanalyst not only may want to have his patient sexually but may also come to love her fully. Conceivable though this turn of events may be, however, it is quite clear that when he is personally unfulfilled, he is neither ready nor equipped, yet, to practice his art—not ready to use his own experience for his patient's best psychological interests, not equipped to structure his inquiry for his patient's experience of psychoanalytic therapy.

Recall, now, the problem of money. If, in the course of every psychoanalytic experience, the patient encounters and deals with observable effects of counteranxiety, counterresistance, countertransference then, it may be asked, why doesn't he bill his psychoanalyst instead? at least for these phases of therapeutic inquiry? The question, here, involves complex attitudes toward money which are not easily clarified in a highly commercial culture that conditions the expert to expect reasonable payment for services rendered. When the patient, in effect, becomes expert enough to deal seriously with his psychoanalyst's unconscious experience, why not also fix a fee for him in the regular procedure? This question probably is most frequently raised by those who are least secure about a patient's growing intuitive awareness and who, on account of this, would prefer to ignore transactive possibilities inherent in attempting an open experience with all patients. To put the answer simply and directly: A patient does not bill his psychoanalyst because, after therapeutic inquiry is under way, counteranxiety, counterresistance, countertransference always become relevant at certain crucial turnings of any patient's psychoanalytic experience. Consequently, his ability to explore and analyze their effects is part of completing the experience as a whole.

Aside from this, moreover, psychoanalytic therapy which succeeds is invaluable and beyond appraisal in monetary terms. When it fails, it is valueless, however, and also beyond appraisal in monetary terms. Of the psychoanalyst, therefore, who asks about compensating a patient for the analysis of counteranxiety, counterresistance, countertransference, it may be asked whether he is also prepared to refund fees in case he fails to accomplish the analysis of transference, resistance, anxiety. Here, of course, the whole fee question quite obviously threatens to become absurd. If any psychoanalyst agreed to this, he would set conditions for practically insuperable resistance to psychoanalytic inquiry. Even in the most classical of procedures, there no doubt are cases in which return of fees could be far more pleasurable, indeed, than success of the therapy. With the patient, for example, who eventually prefers his difficulties in living to disturbances of awareness arising from analysis of anxieties or who encounters new problems in daily life and, to resolve them, simply wants his money back, therapy would develop into a most peculiar risk for the psychoanalyst.

If only for the purpose of taking a direct approach to this problem, practical reason requires that a clean straight line be drawn in psychoanalysis between work done and fees for it. Perhaps the psychoanalyst might first estimate the income he needs to support his way of life and then, apart from any single patient's ability to meet his set fee, scale adjustments up or down in accordance with the particular patient's financial resources. But decisions about finances ought, themselves, to be contingent upon prior and joint decisions to work together because that patient is a good candidate for psychoanalysis and because that psychoanalyst is the right person with whom to do it. After the work is under way on these terms, questions about fee may ordinarily be treated as indicating psychological problems of one sort or another. The rationale is to place the matter of fees in the domain of social experience, apart from both the psychoanalyst's structure of inquiry and his patient's experience of therapy, in this way leaving economic determinations to the marketplace where they belong.

There are critical and significant aspects of psychoanalytic experience which money does not buy. No patient, for example, can compensate a psychoanalyst for sensitivity and concern, curiosity and alertness, tact and wisdom—indeed, dedication and, even, love—for trained willingness to engage in experience and inquiry which may stretch as far and wide as the patient's quest for individuality, truth and freedom. By the same token, no psychoanalyst can compensate the patient who is finally free enough through his therapy to identify those of his psychoanalyst's personal qualities which, he believes, have been evoked by their special relationship—engaging, as well, in experience and inquiry which may stretch as far and wide as the psychoanalyst's quest for individuality, truth and freedom. The range, profundity, openness and sincerity which are still possible in psychoanalysis certainly are not very common experiences of value in highly material and manipulative patterns of culture that encourage a patient to buy psychology the way he buys other goods and services. But psychoanalysis may now, in fact, represent one of the few remaining avenues which are open to certain distorted, disturbed and difficult personalities who still search for ways to communicate and modify their problems.

As a matter of record and without value judgment, it is now clear, the structure of psychoanalysis governs and sustains inquiry into certain areas of experience which, without it, might be lost to their possessors. Perhaps, it could be argued, they might better be lost and, of course, the argument then moves to metapsychology—to, that is, philosophies of experience and theories of value. Perhaps, it could also be argued, as our society becomes increasingly centralized and as human relations are compelled to become increasingly interpersonal, then the covert, the eccentric, the clannish and the darkly familial may lose their customary meaning and function in the furtherance of human existence. And finally, it could perhaps be argued, even the modern quests for soul, self, identity and authenticity will acquire appropriate space in the history of culture and ideas—alongside tribal wanderings of the ancient shepherds, agrarian serfdom of the medieval social order, child and labor exploitation of the industrial revolution—for these modern quests for certainty may be interpreted as symptoms of a gigantic social and cultural birth trauma through our unprecedented revolutions in space and cybernetic technology, mass communications and expanding human rights, and into the atomic age. Enough, however, of this sort of speculation about culture and experience and about possible current metapsychologies of transference, resistance, anxiety. Some may prefer the instinctual or transcendental to the cultural and interpersonal in metapsychology but, no matter the preferred perspective, single or groups of psychoanalysts may still establish their common ground in a common structure of inquiry which, by design, explores and analyzes conscious and unconscious processes and patterns. For psychoanalysis is not to be confused with interpersonal adaptation or social adjustment. Its structure is, first and foremost, psychological inquiry.

At present, there is no single pattern of relatedness and communication to which all psychoanalysts must fit their experience during actual therapeutic inquiry. The structure of this inquiry does nothing more, in fact, than demarcate empirical, systematic and interpretive orders of psychoanalysis. As logical or scientific instrument, it is used to observe and describe, construct and transform, systematize and clarify. But how a particular psychoanalyst uses himself with a particular patient during actual therapeutic inquiry, of course, is not at all a theoretical or scientific issue. Rather, it is directly a function of what he is capable of experiencing; it is a function of the freedom and maturity of his conscious and unconscious relatedness and communication. For he can take transference, resistance, anxiety to define the patient's participation in psychoanalytic inquiry no more seriously than he takes counteranxiety, counterresistance, countertransference which define his own. The extent and power to which he can participate in exploration and analysis of either set of definitions, with therapy in progress, are matters of individual endowment, self-knowledge and training since, to put it as a truism, no psychoanalyst can do anything which is beyond the fundamental range of his personal psychology. In effect, he structures inquiry to discover the genuine limits of personal and interpersonal experience which both he and his patient can finally attain together and, for this reason, he does not fix guidelines to their experience in advance of actual inquiry whose aim is psychoanalytic therapy.

(2) *Inquiry and Therapy*

An ordered structure of inquiry is a very useful tool to have, therefore, in the daily course of psychoanalytic practice. Not the sort which modifies clinical observation for laboratory experimentation by mechanical devices in the experiential field of therapy but which is, instead, a guide and corrective to the conduct of clinical inquiry. Such a structure may be used, first, to distinguish predominantly psychoanalytic phases of therapeutic experience from those which are not even psychological, second, to clarify what is being realized at various stages of actual therapeutic inquiry and, third, to outline a scheme of symbolic representation which depicts the psychoanalytic structure of therapeutic experience. It is not possible, at present, to conceive a structure of inquiry and scheme of symbolic representation which apply in exact and full detail to every case study or, of course, to make their application universal. In a quiet study or calm seminar, it is exciting to speculate about these possibilities but, while treating any particular patient, the psychoanalyst is responsible for the best he can do with the best knowledge he has available. From the fact that no structure is now universal, however, it does not follow that no structure at all can be demarcated. It need not apply to every psychoanalytic patient or all phases of his therapy, moreover, to account for the empirical possibilities and systematic limits of psychoanalysis. Instead, a serial order of inquiry may be demarcated as the structure by which psychoanalysts do, in fact, guide their therapeutic work. This structure would apply in so far, that is, as their work is explicitly or implicitly psychoanalytic, even though their metapsychologies do not agree in general or coincide at every point. It is because psychoanalysts seek intensive study of the human psyche, of course, that they are always compelled to deal with philosophies of experience and theories of value. Yet, on the other hand, because it is not therapy by suggestion and persuasion which weaves moral judgments into a patient's behavior in the guise of treating him psychologically, its structure of inquiry is limited to psychological grounds, formulated in psychological terms, and applied under psychological conditions. In each instance— grounds, terms, conditions—psychology may be empirically and systematically set off from morals. The clinical structure of psychoanalysis may be so described, in this view, as to embrace therapeutic work done under whatever metapsychology. This general view is being taken, not only to prevent certain moral tendencies from turning contemporary psychoanalysis into a new creed but, in addition, to determine the extent to which theory and practice of psychological change can be coordinated before moral judgments are made for therapeutic purposes. The distinction of inquiry from therapy may be proposed, now, so that inquiry denotes the empirical and systematic orders, and therapy integrates them with that of interpretation and speculation to yield individual psychoanalytic experience—on the assumption that a special structure of inquiry governs the special experience of this therapy. Structure of inquiry is being distinguished from experience of therapy, then, to parallel the

distinction in psychoanalysis of psychology from metapsychology or, in a larger sense, from philosophy and values. These
distinctions, however, are no more important than, and do not
extend beyond, that between structure of inquiry and expe-
rience of therapy. It is within the context of these distinctions that a structure
may be formulated for psychoanalytic inquiry. Although their
metapsychology here derives from the emerging perspectives
of scientific humanism, psychoanalysts with other metapsychologies can also use the structure which is outlined in Chapter 2 and developed in Chapter 3. Its definitions are empirical,
its postulates are broad, its theory is powerful—enough to be
used, profitably, by any psychotherapist interested in psychoanalytic inquiry. Regardless, then, of anyone's preferences in
metapsychology, if his work is implicitly or explicitly psychoanalytic, it shares uniformities with that of psychoanalysts who
may just as well have other such preferences. The problem,
here, is to demarcate the uniformities of their structure of inquiry. Yet psychoanalysis is neither a bourgeois nor a blue-
collar science; nor is it a platform for revolution or conformity.
If patients with metapsychologies other than those now articulated in psychoanalysis—and even, indeed, patients who pro-
fess to have none—are to feel free about undertaking intensive
study of their personal psychology, a thin yet consistent line
must be drawn between general structure of inquiry and particular experiences of therapy. The psychoanalyst works directly
and personally to understand a patient without certain fore-
knowledge, in each case, that he can interpret any other person's
psychology wholly in terms of his own metapsychology. Since
interpretation finally depends on metapsychology, each participant is free to reconstruct both his philosophy and values to
suit his psychology and his psychology to suit his philosophy
and values. But their common purpose remains, throughout,

empirical and systematic analysis of psychological processes and patterns. This approach may make the work harder, but it also makes the results clearer. It eventually hits the hard question, what are psychoanalytic facts? There is nothing invidious in the distinction of facts from theories or fictions, as these terms are now used in philosophy of science[4]; and no attempt is therefore being made to sketch a perspective on the patient's psychoanalytic experience in accordance with such metapsychological terms as, for example, the relations of organism and environment. For no matter the perspective—instinctual dialectics, struggle for power, collective unconscious, pure will and so on—it is still necessary to demarcate empirical and systematic boundaries of structured inquiry in clinical psychoanalysis. If it turns out, moreover, that this sort of approach cannot be adopted and realized, then no perspective on metapsychology has empirical legs or systematic grounds. The point is, briefly, to designate the hard facts of psychoanalytic inquiry under whatever metapsychology.

Nor does this approach aim to produce a step-by-step guide to the actual conduct of psychoanalysis. At present, no such guide is either practical or necessary. Until men become or are treated as machines, furthermore, it is pointless to attempt outlines of procedure which so well transcend individual differences that they invariably yield the facts of psychoanalytic inquiry. Beyond this, finally, there still are no substitutes for both the skill and alertness and the tact and wisdom required to carry out psychoanalytic inquiry in the shared experience of therapy. If it is possible, then, to determine how these inquiries are psychoanalytic, and if it is possible to demarcate their structure, psychoanalysts of all metapsychologies—both publicly defended and privately cherished—may approach agreement on empirical terms and systematic transformations which they adopt in common. They may also find it possible to establish a reasonable basis for resolving disagreements in meta-psychology outside the field of actual clinical inquiry. If it does not prove possible to establish this structure, however, its empirical and systematic objectives will have to be pursued in still other structures, and its interpretive and speculative objectives may yet be attained on moral, religious and philosophic grounds, or eventually be superseded by new perspectives on morals, religion and philosophy. This issue disturbs psychoanalysts of all known metapsychological persuasions, and their responses to it range from the projection of hypothetico-deductive systems, to organized efforts at experimental and psycho-computer assessments of psychoanalytic "data"—in quotation, at this point, because their definitive features remain to be specified—to absurdist and mystical resolutions by the ahistorical leap into absolute transcendence.

The attempt is to explore the structure of psychoanalytic facts, however, on the assumption that it can be done within the experiential limits of therapeutic inquiry. To this end, three notions are basic: first, the experiential field of therapy which is the root source and operative field of all psychotherapies; second, the experience of psychoanalytic therapy which results from transformations of this field of therapy in accordance with the structure of psychoanalytic inquiry; and third, the psychoanalytic structure by means of which it is possible to observe, define, transform, explain and interpret. In other words, this structure is applied to the experiential field of therapy when both psychoanalyst and patient seek its objectives and when its objectives are within the range of the psychoanalyst's training, the patient's competence and their mutual interest. In terms of these three notions, psychoanalytic experience may be said to result from a distinctively psychoanalytic resolution of the psychological problem originally presented in the experiental field of therapy. If, instead, a structure of short-term, nondirective, hypnotic or other inquiry is applied, then the therapeutic experience respectively becomes short-term, nondirective, hypnotic or other. And if, by the same token, the structure of psychoanalytic inquiry is applied in the id model, the ego or interpersonal model or the model of shared experience—exclusively, consecutively or in any of their many possible combinations and variations—it is also proposed that psychoanalytic resolutions do not escape the interpretive limits of the special model in which they are attained. For systematic purposes, however, definitions, postulates and theory may be formulated in terms general enough to cut across the interpretive metapsychology of each clinical model and, also, particular enough to encompass varieties of psychoanalytic fact at the foundation of all three.

In addition to the previously mentioned need for sharper differentiation of psychology from values in the course of the actual work, this structure of inquiry responds, as well, to the need for greater clarity about the respective contributions of both participants to the whole experience. If this need can be successfully answered, perhaps psychoanalysts will be able to work with far less concern for nonconformities and alienations, and then gear inquiry to psychological results without getting locked into their patient's social and moral dilemmas. Ordinarily, successful conformists do not value psychological change or seek psychoanalytic experience. These persons are not easily persuaded to change, after all, until they are forced into it by social and cultural circumstance but, as successful conformists, they most likely change unawares to get along within their new behavioral environment. Only when their conformities begin to break down—they, in effect, becoming nonconformists too—do they call a psychoanalyst. No matter, then, whether we are all insane as our society or schizoid as our culture, it is still possible even for conformists who break down to explore what they still may reasonably hope to become. But the disturbed nonconformist's problem differs, however, because he has not yet been able to make the adjustment. Of course, he may want to remain nonconformist after the psychoanalytic work is done but, as long as he actually becomes more capable of awareness and knowledge which directly affect his behavior, his adjustment need not especially concern the psychoanalyst.

It is rather narrow and constricting, moreover, for any psychoanalyst in this dawning age of atomic energy, space and cybernetic technology, mass communications and expanding human rights to persist in the thorough application of metapsychologies which were produced and lived by his late nineteenth-century predecessors. The purpose of distinguishing psychology from values, psychology from metapsychology, structure of inquiry from experience of therapy, is neither to prize and purify the one side of this series nor to deny and condemn the other. The purpose of these distinctions is to make possible a full and reliable study of either side without also having constantly to refer to the other—even though as naturalistic event, clearly, one is never explored in the other's total absence. Working within the special limits and possibilities of his structure of inquiry, the psychoanalyst may enjoy far greater confidence in his psychoanalytic judgment than he can ever expect to attain in moral judgment, since many subtle differences and gross disagreements about values may rightfully arise between himself and his patient when he practices his therapeutic art in a free society.

Over the last sixty years, the focus of psychoanalytic theory has expanded to the point of reversing itself. Psychoanalysts, today, agree far more about the therapeutic significance of transference, resistance, anxiety and counteranxiety, counterresistance, countertransference than they do, or ever did, about

the metapsychology of these disturbed and distorted processes
and patterns. In 1910, for example, Freud used the principle
of psychosexuality to define psychoanalysis, in sharp contrast
to the practice of a wild and essentially wrong psychoanalytic
technique.[5] Nearly twenty years later, however, Reich was introducing his pioneer seminar on character analysis at the
Vienna Institute with the observation that there were about
as many individual procedures as psychoanalysts[6]—who no
longer practiced wildly and, presumably, had become well
seasoned. Yet, in 1928, he also claimed metapsychology as the
main thread of unity among them. Not a structure of therapeutic inquiry, because it still lacked consistent formulation,
but a special perspective on metapsychology—ideology, that is,
or philosophy of experience and value—was his recommended
source and support of the foundations of psychoanalysis. Char-
acter-analytic therapy as well, of course, as ego and interpersonal
therapy were all serious and constructive responses to this
problem, converging from different perspectives on metapsychology. Instead, however, of hanging the foundations from
conflicting metapsychologies and, in this way, weakening their
therapeutic power, they may well be fastened more securely to
structure of inquiry at their empirical and systematic base.
It is being assumed that the current stalemate in psychoanalysis
largely results from a curious blindness to this fundamental
change—an assumption which need not be demonstrated, here,
because success in this new direction will so transform current
theory and practice as to make such demonstrations the concern of practicing historians rather than practicing psychoanalysts. To this end, a structure of inqury has to be formulated which demarcates empirical and systematic orders of
psychoanalytic inquiry and which leaves interpretive metapsychology to its radically pluralistic fate for all particular and, in
some sense, unique therapeutic experiences. To stand psycho-

analysis on its structure of inquiry—on, so to speak, its feet—it is necessary to acknowledge that, at present, there is no possibility of overcoming the wide gaps of opinion among psychoanalysts over metapsychology. But it is possible to affirm, fortunately, that psychoanalysts and patients may disagree about issues in philosophy and value and still cooperate in a psychoanalytic structure to guide the conduct of their therapeutic inquiries.

(3) *Models of Therapy*

Recall the three models of therapy through which the special structure of psychoanalytic inquiry can now be applied—those of the id, the ego or interpersonal relations, and shared experience. These are the major models which have so far been outlined. They are all applicable and fruitful, it is proposed, in accordance with their respective metapsychologies, for the three are intimately related. But they are not held mutually exclusive. Rather, they are equally valid and, as long as their metapsychologies are carefully aligned with their funded observations, they may even become complementary. The id model has been well known since around 1915, and the ego or interpersonal model has also been well known since its various descriptions from about 1928 through 1940, while the transactional model of shared experience is still in the process of being formulated.[7]

The first model corresponds to innovations of id therapy in which the relevance of definitions, postulates and theory to specific clinical observations was only tentatively understood. Their relevance was recognized, of course, as both arising from and referring back to observable processes and patterns but, because of interpretive excesses of one particular slant in metapsychology, the relations among them were not always kept clear and distinct. Nor, indeed, were they seen to apply beyond the particular model of therapy in which they were originally formulated. Some fragmentary structure of inquiry, although but vaguely worked out, was conceived as supporting conclusions from therapy of the id with a limited number and type of patient—the so-called transference neurosis. In this early model, postulates of genesis and dynamism were most frequently applied to the operational definitions of transference and resistance, while the sexual theory of personality development was almost universally applied beyond psychology. Acknowledged to exist on parallel grounds, countertransference and counter-resistance were both pointedly excluded from the experiential field of id therapy because, in this model, any significant involvement of psychoanalyst and patient could be conceived only as sexual and aggressive at the instinctual level, and the resulting interlock would clearly make it practically impossible for psychological inquiry to achieve clarification, resolution and reconstruction of distortion, disturbance and difficulty.

The second model corresponds to formulations of ego or interpersonal therapy for which the definition of resistance—or, in other terms, character armor, defense mechanism, security operation—was given greater emphasis to make similar observations from the various perspectives in which each term was used. On the basis of later evidence, these terms were worked down to a uniform definition. They became more reliable and they were also applied with far greater specificity and consistency. During this phase, they became, as it were, more muscular. To coordinate the structure of psychoanalytic inquiry further, there were attempts to supplement analysis of id transference with that of ego transference, distinguish the genuine more sharply from the distorted in the therapeutic experience of transference and resistance, and develop new perspectives on metapsychology. In this ego or interpersonal model, postulates of function and structure were specifically emphasized, moreover, as counterparts to those of genesis and dynamism. These postulates were applied to the analysis of transference and, for the first time, also to the analysis of resistance as observable process and pattern but, above all, to a growing concern with clinical manifestations of anxiety. To accomplish these postulate transformations, the ego or interpersonal psychoanalyst viewed himself as a participant observer who used the method of interpersonal relations in the experiential field of therapy. As participant observer, however, his counteranxiety now became as significant an operational definiton as counterresistance and countertransference but, as professional expert, he still was not to be openly observed and described as well, however, by his co-participant observer in the interpersonal field because, most likely, he did not entrust himself to his patient's experience.

The third model corresponds, roughly, to developments of therapy of shared experience in which definitions, postulates and theory reinforce one another in a systematic structure. Its reliability, as a whole, is confirmed by the more or less recurrent and remote observations it supports in shared fields of therapeutic experience. At the present stage of its formulation, psychoanalytic structure may appear to assume a deductive cast because of the internal relations of its orders of inquiry or, more simply, because of perhaps irrepressible strivings for deductive systematics. The most significant thing about it for both research and therapy is, it never becomes purely deductive without failing as organized inquiry into actual experience, or wholly intuitive without moving into the domain of pure logic and mysticism. New evidence of empirical observations may now and then enlarge and modify the propositions of this structure, but neither single nor accumulated observations can destroy it. They help only to remold it. Psychoanalysis of experience in the field of its occurrence is here to stay, of course; and in this third model, the field of shared experience itself becomes a major subject of interest. With two new postulates of immediacy or affect and reflection or cognition, the psychoanalyst is now willing to undertake reconstructive study of distorted experience no matter when and how it comes to be observed, no matter who possesses or defines it, no matter what its original sources or actual objectives—within the limits, to be sure, of his personal psychology and metapsychology. He now also applies definitions of transference, resistance, anxiety together with those of counteranxiety, counterresistance, countertransference under the original and actual conditions of their observation. For the first time, too, he aims to distinguish interpretive metapsychologies as clearly and consistently as possible from empirical and systematic orders of inquiry. Chief among the reasons for doing this are, first, to single out theory of unconscious experience as his integrative explanation of psychological problems,[8] second, to show how his structure of clinical inquiry is compatible with diverse philosophies of experience and theories of value and, third, to make it possible for him to demarcate this structure in psychological rather than moralistic terms.

Earlier, in hypnocathartic therapy for example, the observations, definitions, transformations, explanations and interpretations had been contracted into simple generalizations from particular cases. Consider observations which supported the notion of hypnoid states. After it was observed that selected processes and patterns presenting certain recurrent characteristics, c_n, also presented certain other recurrent characteristics, c'_n, it was concluded that observations of c' tended to follow those of c—that as the patient discussed and serially abreacted psychological symptoms, they tended one by one to disappear. The method of this early phase is generalization from particular cases, supported and refined by both positive and negative instances, and its results are still valid for the clinical conditions under which they were first obtained. But therapy has since undergone radical change to the point where hypnocatharsis is no longer related in theory or practice to psychoanalysis—except, of course, in the sense of historical antecedence—and to the point where the notion of hypnoid states has gradually been refined into a theory of unconscious experience that now circumscribes the empirical range of psychoanalytic structure.

At present, postulates and theory of psychoanalysis are viewed as interweaving to form systematic orders which bear upon the observed and defined particulars of gross experience.[9] In this way, reconstruction of earlier hypnocathartic therapy, together with more recent observations and postulates, have shaped the structure of inquiry. They are now so well ordered into a working structure of observation, definition, postulate and theory that alterations of any one constituent require coordinating alterations of the others. In addition, they also form a structure as to support each other in demarcating the psychoanalytic field of inquiry. While remaining relevant to the actual experience of therapy, these orders of inquiry may sometimes appear to be deductive, especially when relations of definition to both postulate and theory are not kept clearly distinct from its relations to metapsychology. But psychoanalysis no longer is merely concerned with deriving its generalizations from observations of gross experience. It is also concerned, at present, with systematic aspects of its inquiry, even though it is not and cannot in fact become a purely deductive science. Empirical observation retains a responsible status of its own, and continues to provide the transactional moorings of psychoanalytic knowledge. All observation, however, remains subject both to enlargement as empirical structure widens its base and to reinterpretation as systematic structure reworks its limits. Despite the unarguable principle, in any case, that general theory and empirical practice guide and control one another, the central question still remains. Since no observation includes all particular processes and patterns, how is it possible to determine that this proposed structure, and this one alone, is most appropriate to the facts and theory of psychoanalytic inquiry? The answer is, in brief, that its appropriateness is established primarily in terms of emipirical observations which have already been made and coordinated. Among other things, this implies that structure of psychoanalytic inquiry is provisional and open, that psycho-analytic knowledge is also provisional and tentative and, above all, that many problems remain to be explored and resolved in both the transformation and the explanation of defined ob-servations.

Historically, of course, the biological Freudians first de-veloped the model of id therapy. They worked out a nonpar-ticipant view of psychoanalytic observation, reinforced it with mirror psychology and, then, did not favorably regard either interactive or transactive experience in the field of therapy. The ego and interpersonal therapists, as either biological or cultural Freudians, or as both, later modified this model to acknowledge genuine empirical effects of the psychoanalyst's personal style of observation. But they lacked a unified view of the experiential field of therapy. They still did not consider the psychoanalyst as actively participating to produce the very ex-perience in and through which he can openly observe and be observed—within the limits and the possibilities, to be sure, of both his and his patient's personalities. As one significant con-sequence of this, he remained the participant observer of ego or interpersonal therapy and did not freely become, in turn, an observed participant during shared psychoanalytic experience—taking the attitude, instead, that it was he and not his patient who qualified as expert in the study of interpersonal relations. Although these two models of therapy were originally designed to achieve fundamental changes in personal psychology, they

often produced intellectual and defensive readjustments of behavior instead. Perhaps, it may be said in retrospect, these
readjustments were to protect patient and psychoanalyst against
emotional complexities arising from the one's shared experience
of the other. In the id model, for example, the patient tended
to produce a string of ruminative associations about childhood
sexuality which were in some sense free, perhaps, but in no
clear sense liberating. Or in the ego or interpersonal model,
the patient tended to secure defensive distance by analyzing the
transference of defense mechanisms or tracing the distortion of
security operations, instead of concentrating his efforts on what
he had to armor, defend or secure himself against. And in both,
the patient was then obliged to refer all processes and patterns
of relatedness and communication back to the development and
function of his own personality. But if, as the various metapsychologies of both models do assert, severe distortion, disturbance and difficulty often originate and flourish in shared
fields of experience—during crucial phases of infancy, early and
later childhood, preadolescence, early and later adolescence, or
even adulthood—then, to be effective about such psychological
problems, the psychoanalyst also has to reflect and respond to
this genesis and structure in so far, at least, as his field of
therapy actually subtends shared experience with another person, the patient. If, in other words, the patient has genuinely
new and meaningful perception of his psychoanalyst's private
and unconscious experience, to the extent at least that he per-
ceives it impinging on his own, there is no theoretical or practical reason to prevent all living traces of this significant event
from touching his psychoanalyst—not on grounds, at any rate,
of a therapeutic model.

In the model of shared experience,[10] psychoanalysis is conceived and practiced as inquiry into the therapeutic field of
experience and transaction. The whole range of a patient's

experience as it converges and intertwines with the psycho-analyst's is, for the first time, defined and transformed, explained and interpreted. To this end, transactions of shared experience themselves become a source of reliable and warranted observations of transference, resistance, anxiety and counteranxiety, counterresistance, countertransference—and not a source of duplicates, copies or representatives of outside live experience. Although these two clusters of definition are used in all three models to define selected processes and patterns, when applied in the model of shared experience, their range of application is enlarged to extend through actual and potential transactions of both participants. Over the last sixty years, statement of these definitions has gradually evolved through different approaches to their current usage in the model of shared experience. At present, it is proposed, the genetic approach of id therapy combines with the functional approach of ego or interpersonal therapy and, as a genetic-functional approach, also encompass future expectations. That is, the outgoing past, the ongoing present and the incoming future are viewed as integrated aspects of a single psycho-analytic approach, while processes and patterns of personal psychology are being treated as unitary manifestations of particular persons who happen to share the experience of therapeutic inquiry.

Undergoing shared experience, then, both psychoanalyst and patient are active co-participants in inquiry such that the experiences and activities of one may become appropriate matters of perception and judgment by the other. The role of the patient's is practically self-evident, of course, because his distortion, disturbance and difficulty provide the initial motive and context of his therapeutic work. But a psychoanalyst also contributes far more to the endeavor than metaphors of mirror, expert or partner suggest, selecting some observations of gross

experience for definition, transformation, explanation and interpretation, ignoring others because they are not readily
specified by definition and transformed by postulate or are not
clearly explained by theory and interpreted by his perspective
on metapsychology, noticing some without being able to do
more than invite his patient's attention and curiosity, failing
to notice others which do not penetrate beyond his counteranxiety, counterresistance, countertransference—all these activities emanating, obviously, from the operant conditions of a
psychoanalyst's psychology and metapsychology. With them, he
attempts to work through the mirror of impersonal profes-
sionalism, beyond the interpersonal distance of ego defenses,
toward open study of indefinite varieties of transference, resistance, anxiety converging with equally indefinite varieties of
counteranxiety, counterresistance, countertransference, as these
intertwine at the growing edge of shared psychoanalytic experience. The range of their inquiry expands, accordingly, to
include for close study shared experiences which are formed
and which can be transformed by, essentially, its co-participants.
The special point, here, is that once involved, psychoanalyst and
patient make it together in some ways even to the point of defining the one's experiential compass by his relatedness and
communication to the other. The psychoanalyst need no longer
limit inquiry to resolution of symptoms, external change of
behavior, or reinterpretation of metapsychology, especially with
a patient who is not interested in narrow goals of hypnotic,
supportive or reeducative psychotherapies. Rather, he may now
involve himself far more directly than a mirror, expert or
partner in making the psychoanalytic experience. He may involve himself continuously and cumulatively in sharing the inquiry, not only to help a patient become aware of his unconscious experience but, in so doing, also to become aware of his
own processes newly emerged and patterns newly formed in

response to his patient's newly emerged processes and newly formed patterns.

To work with a patient in this model, the psychoanalyst begins with himself. He does not need to use tape recorders and other mechanical devices, take notes while sessions are in progress or do anything else which could interfere with his full attention and occupation in the therapeutic experience. As he tries to follow any communication of whatever source, content or objective, he wants to hear a patient's presentation of himself, his problem and his understanding of it. He is not committed to attempting, then, to establish the superiority or inadequacy of any school of metapsychology or any one postulate's relations to the others and, beyond them, to other orders of the structure. Stresses and strains in the patient's presentation of himself and his problem, form and content of the transactions which develop from his psychoanalyst's responses to him and his problem and, in turn, develop from his responses to his psychoanalyst and to his responses, and so on—these create a rhythmic flow of collaborative inquiry to which the psychoanalyst attempts to apply his definitions, postulates, theory and metapsychology that make up the structure of psychoanalysis. For when some intermittent impression obtained of his patient's problem begins to acquire the form of a recurrent pattern of experience, it is gained and generalized through focused efforts of the whole range of a psychoanalyst's personal psychology—strivings and feelings, thoughts and fantasies, needs and goals and ideals, as these combine in his conscious and unconscious experience; and the same holds true, of course, for the patient's impressions of his psychoanalyst. Every psychoanalytic therapy reflects the special ways a particular psychoanalyst uses his experience with a particular patient and a particular patient uses his experience with a particular psychoanalyst. In this sense, it is inevitably personal and concrete.

With a common structure of inquiry, psychoanalysts may join together in distinguishing their special type of psycho-therapy from other psychotherapies—short-term, nondirective, hypnotic and so on. But each particular psychoanalyst develops a concrete field of therapy with each particular patient and, under the special conditions of psychoanalytic structure, their joint inquiry may lead to unique experiential outcomes. Even though this structure may be generalized to include the work of all psychoanalysts, each one's work with each of his patients falls into characteristic rhythms which he learns are best suited to his temperament, personality and metapsychology, and most useful for effective collaboration with that patient. In any case, he is as open to each of his patients as his own unconscious ex-perience permits, yet he cannot deny his patient the communi-cation of new insights about it, especially when these insights openly emerge and apply most penetratingly to his unconscious experience of that patient. He may discourage and, of course, even prohibit a patient's open expression of such responses to counteranxiety, counterresistance, countertransference. But—and this is the point—he cannot actually prevent a patient from having them in the experiential field of therapy or from eval-uating them in private and in silence. If he did openly prohibit their expression, moreover, he would then have to be prepared for varieties of disguise and defense by which a patient may re-spond to the psychoanalyst's inability to hear new insights about himself. As a rule, therefore, he does not even discourage the open expression and analysis of new insights which are most concerned about his own participation in shared experience.

Most important by far, however, this third model broadens the field of inquiry. It affirms psychoanalytic experience as both live and continuous and temporal and cumulative related-ness and communication, as itself a whole experience—a kind of history in the making, as it were, with beginning, middle and end—not only for every patient but for every psychoanalyst as well. In this model, all observation and definition take place within the context of shared experience. Their transformation, explanation and interpretation also take place within it and, then, are to be referred back to it. No void or vacuum need be posited, therefore, for the patient's experience of his psychoanalyst—nor, indeed, the other way around—and no mirror or screen need be interposed between the two co-participants. Nor, of course, need any sector of their relations be considered more inter than personal or, as in some recent existentialisms, more transcendent than immanent. Exploration and analysis of psychoanalytic observation, in other words, does not lose track of itself in infinite regress to past history, and it does not encircle itself within unconscious defenses of the specious present. During reconstructive movements of therapy, it is proposed instead, as a patient becomes better acquainted with undiscovered aspects of himself, the psychoanalyst also has to become better acquainted with appropriately responsive aspects of his own self in order to receive or, at the least, register changes in his patient's relatedness and communication. In response, the patient then has to introduce appropriate aspects of himself in order to receive or, at the least again, register changes in his psychoanalyst's relatedness and communication. Otherwise, reconstruction of the one's scope of awareness cannot join in mutual reconstruction of the other's and, as a result, therapeutic movement turns back upon itself and into antecedent patterns of response to sustain essential continuity of their shared experience. Distorted relatedness is, indeed, better than none, and this judgment may be said to hold true for any psychoanalytic metapsychology since, no matter how distorted the relatedness and communication may be during inquiry, it still holds genuine promise of reconstruction.

A model of shared experience need not discard firm empirical results obtained in mirror therapy of the id, interpersonal therapy of the ego defenses or variations related to them. This model is not being exclusively set forth, then, as the most accurate, precise or valid, since all three have established claims to accuracy, precision and validity, and in no case need firm empirical results be discarded. But since this model also makes full clinical observations in terms of transference, resistance, anxiety and counteranxiety, counterresistance, countertransference, supports the study of their transactions in ways which other models do not specify yet, at the same time, does not violate recurrent observations which they do make, it enlarges the structure and expands the experience of psychoanalysis. Consistent with their respective conditions, each model is at least self-supporting and may even be considered complementary to the others and all, of course, are valid within their limits of metapsychology. No single model is exhaustive, however, or exclusive—each by its own perspective confining the experiential field of therapy to its special fund of evidence from the seething cauldron of the id, the operation of ego or interpersonal defenses, the transactions of shared experience. All three can eventually become a coordinated body of knowledge, providing that no one obscures another's critical meaning by simple appropriation of empirical and systematic findings. In accordance with individual preferences in metapsychology and, indeed, implicitly or explicitly, they actually are modified in terms of one another because, used alone, they impose artificial limits on the conduct of psychoanalytic therapy.

For all models, furthermore, psychoanalytic structure works in temporal contexts of the present which are bounded by recall of the past and a foresight of the future, both conscious and unconscious. Seeking the best which is consistent with the possible, this structure of definition, postulate and theory governs observation of gross experience and, then, either modifies formulations of structure in accordance with enlarged fields of inquiry or enlarges fields of inquiry in accordance with modified formulations of structure. Its systematic orders of postuation and theory remain broadly probable on the basis of its empirical orders of observation and definition. But interpretive metapsychology controls neither observation and definition nor postulation and theory with greater power than any aspect of observation and definition controls postulations and theory, or with greater power than any aspect of postulation and theory controls observation and definition. This, schematically, is how the distinction of psychology from metapsychology sets in psychoanalysis. The present structure differs sharply from its historical antecendents, however, in that the probabilities of its inquiry no longer fluctuate as radically with the appearance of new evidence and no longer require as full a reconstruction of the whole of its structure. Its systematic orders already form a structure such that it can no longer be said to become simply more or less true as a whole but, rather, somewhat more or somehow less coherent, inclusive, reliable. Especially by distinguishing empirical and systematic psychology from interpretive metapsychology, however, does this structure of psychoanalytic inquiry yield experiences of psychoanalytic therapy in particular through experiential fields of therapy in general.[11] It attempts to fulfill at least one aim of science, a structure of inquiry which exhibits systematic order within itself and guides empirical observation of gross experience—whose processes and patterns, here, are distorted in perception, disturbed in awareness, difficult in living.

B. BEFORE METAPSYCHOLOGY

Since metapsychologies do not distinguish structures of inquiry from one another, there is no real point to classifying psychotherapists in accordance with their many perspectives on metapsychology. From a particular psychoanalyst's adoption of one or another perspective, it is no longer possible to infer the structure of his therapeutic inquiry with patients. What he must adopt, as well, is a structure of inquiry which guides the empirical and systematic study of psychological problems toward a distinctively psychoanalytic experience. It is in this sense that psychoanalytic structure logically precedes metapsychology. For it may be demarcated to include no more than that which becomes available in psychoanalytic inquiry—the processes and patterns which are studied by its direct means— leaving other structures of inquiry to those best qualified to demarcate them in their respective experiences of therapy and leaving metapsychologies to those best situated in the sciences and humanities to construct philosophies of experience. In this respect, however, psychoanalytic structure is no different from short-term, nondirective, hypnotic and the other structures of therapeutic inquiry in that it acquires a perspective on metapsychology only as it is explicitly extended to include philosophy of experience. This means, in effect, that the relation of transference and resistance may be treated as an empirical and systematic proposition because all therapists working toward psychoanalytic experience subscribe to it, while the relations of transference to instinctual dialectics, struggle for power, collective unconscious, pure will and so on represent some of the better known options at the interpretive order.

This view of psychoanalysis points to the definition and transformation of its empirical base without prematurely introducing a priori allegiances to partisan metapsychologies. The therapeutic situation is already well stabilized: psychoanalysts of various perspectives on metapsychology, with at least as much enthusiasm as their patients, report a favorable percentage of positive results. If this is true, however, perhaps lines separating the true from the false in ongoing therapeutic work have little or no direct correlation with lines separating the many schools, disciplines and associations from one another. Since, in fact, all psychotherapy involves philosophies of experience, it is important to be able to demarcate as inquiry significant conditions of observation, definition, transformation and explanation which ground the experience of psychoanalytic therapy and in whose presence, as well, the structure is properly psychoanalytic rather than other psychological or therapeutic inquiries. The focus of this study, then, does not spread to the significance of every psychology and therapy; it is being kept steady on the perspective, process and product of psychoanalysis.

In conducting therapy, well trained psychoanalysts of various metapsychologies continue to observe and define relatively similar processes and patterns of relatedness and communication. Perhaps because of this, if for no other reason, they can now lay aside differences in philosophy and terminology without, however, affecting either the common structure of their inquiry or the varieties of experience in which they participate. The point, of course, is to begin assorting the vast body of hunches, observations, operational terms, postulations, theory and metapsychologies in which is embedded the special experience that distinguishes psychoanalysis from other psychotherapies. As a direct result of increased clarity about transference, resistance, anxiety and counteranxiety, counterresistance, countertransference, this has become far more feasible than ever before and, in addition, may be far more productive than endless dispute over the interpretive and speculative issues. Recent work in systematic theory suggests, furthermore, that psychoanalysis has settled new frontiers in psychology and may already be strong enough to abandon closed dogmas of cultism for patterns of free inquiry.

The current profusion of metapsychologies calls for an ordered structure of inquiry which, to the extent that it proves possible, cuts across parochialisms of belief without violating integrities of fact. In order to demarcate this structure, does it suffice to treat psychoanalysis as a study of relations among certain specifiable patterns and processes which may then be transformed in a systematic way? Although perspectives on metapsychology are often partisan in the extreme, the structure of inquiry itself is now capable of clearer description than heretofore: It has outgrown exclusive concern with the vicissitudes of infantile libido; it has gone beyond the bifurcation of transference into infantile libido and ego or character defense; it now identifies the two as inseparable aspects of unitary patterns of the whole range of personal psychology in relatedness and communication, and frames its empirical and systematic questions, increasingly, in terms of particular shared experiences through which psychoanalysts meet patients for therapeutic purposes. As organized inquiry, in this view, psychoanalytic structure does not stand or fall in accordance with the passing fortunes of any single set of personal beliefs and social values.

If investigators believe that interpreted human psychology is instinctual dialectics, struggle for power, collective unconscious, pure will and so on, they in no way reshape the empirical and systematic structure of the inquiry. Since beliefs and values of the various metapsychologies neither are nor need be formulated as scientific psychology, their followers may at least agree upon an ordered structure of psychoanalytic inquiry. For if these radical differences were or, indeed, could be formulated as scientific psychology, they might already have become tractable and, in a critical sense, opened to resolution. Over sixty years of psychoanalytic inquiry have not yet made this possible, and it is not reasonable to expect it to happen, therefore, in the immediate or proximate future. Psychoanalytic metapsychologists still prefer to couch their disagreements in vigorous and somewhat bitter polemic—at times engaging, even, in the public therapy of their opposition—yet they do not seek the powerful animus of modern political religions and, fortunately, are not committed to life-and-death struggles with their opposite numbers. These disagreements do not arise, strictly, from differing structures of empirical and systematic inquiry. They arise, rather, from conflicting philosophies of life, about which there is still room to differ among rational men. Thus, practicing psychoanalysts need only agree to allow for such differences among themselves and with their patients for, as psychoanalysts, they are no more confused or less gifted than every man addressing the larger philosophic issues. Besides, no psychoanalyst can regard established metapsycologies as absolute in number or exhaustive in meaning but only as representative of the whole range now in actual use. In fact, no two psychoanalysts can affirm any single philosophy of experience to the last iota, and still retain a clear sense of their particular identities as mature persons.

As observed and described, therefore, psychological processes and patterns still do not invariably manifest any fixed instincts or power struggles, universal archetypes or pure wills. Nor, yet, have they clearly required such categories of interpretation—except, of course, through the agency of certain psychoanalytic metapsychologies. There still are no fixed hierarchies of value, furthermore, which govern the therapeutic action of psychoanalysis as it is actually observed to occur. No therapeutic experience, obviously, is a matter of serious psychoanalytic inquiry before it comes into actual existence but, afterward, any absolute value which either participant ascribes to its results constricts for both the movement of imaginative intelligence. The several metapsychologies of psychoanalysis are, thus, interpretive and speculative. Their function in any one type of psychotherapy does not essentially differ in kind from their function in any other. In actual practice, the differences are those of personal accent and emphasis, depending as much for their enactment on the particular psychoanalyst's funded and fundamental beliefs as on his avowed metapsychology. About human experience and values, in other words, there is nothing substantive he can say in psychoanalytic inquiry which he cannot say about them in, for example, short-term, nondirective or hypnotic therapy—or, for that matter, in difficult situations of daily life. To the extent, then, that every man has a philosophy of life, no matter how naïve and unfinished, he also has the makings of psychoanalytic metapsychology. And every psychoanalyst has one as well, it is proposed, whether or not he follows any which are now institutionalized as schools of thought or through professional association. To assert that structure of psychoanalytic inquiry is not directly dependent on any single metapsychology, of course, is not the same as asserting the probability of favorable results without any metapsychology altogether. Neither psychoanalyst nor patient could so live his life or, indeed, even work with the other. But since the practice of psychoanalysis is still a peculiar blend of science and art, however, that part which is structure of inquiry should have its own organized statement, leaving artistry of its application to the tact, alertness and wisdom of each practitioner who is then free to work out his individual and, in vital respects, induplicative blend.

There are general questions in psychoanalytic inquiry, then, concerning the structure of observation, definition, postulation and theory. When obtained and checked in the field of therapy, answers to these questions point the way to far more reliable order and application of psychoanalytic knowledge. With this firm scientific base, moreover, gathered information can be more easily sorted for theory and practice. It is also probable, furthermore, that confusions of analysis in which high orders of interpretation are prematurely introduced, for example, to explain wishes and intentions not yet evident in actual observation may be at least minimized, if not entirely avoided. To these ends, the center of therapeutic interest turns away from speculative interpretation of experience and value over to empirical and systematic inquiry, away from metapsychology over to psychology. In contrast to preconceived schemes of metapsychology, this shift in focus emphasizes the primacy of genuine psychological knowledge. What methodological change does it bring about in psychoanalysis? The view, in brief, that psychological processes and patterns not only define but are also defined by their psychoanalytic field of experience and, therefore, that no single metapsychology supports the conduct of inquiry in this field. It is to participate in this therapeutic inquiry, then, that the psychoanalyst keeps his own judgments of value distinct from his patient's—not such general values as individuality, truth and freedom about which both participants may easily agree but, rather, middle-range values of what to work at and whom to marry, how to raise and educate children, where to live and when to take vacations, and so on about which they may even greatly differ and still be able to work together. In the structure of psychoanalysis, it is thus proposed that philosophies of experience and value be placed at the interpretive order of inquiry. No matter how broad or integrated, then, this order is not the special stuff of which the psychoanalyst makes his therapeutic inquiry empirical or systematic. And neither, of course, does the mere acquisition of one established metapsychology or another make his inquiry psychoanalytic. Consider, for example, the frequency with which the avowed Freudian in metapsychology—biological, ego or interpersonal, psychological—does not practice psychoanalytic or, in some cases, any other psychological therapy. It is his use of a special structure in the conduct of a special inquiry to a special experience which, rather, makes his work psychoanalytic. This is a hard fact of all scientific efforts in this field even though, in therapeutic inquiry as in daily life, metapsychology sets the interpretive and speculative range of personal fulfillment.

Chapter 2

Structure of Inquiry I

BASIC TO ANY FIELD of science are the existence and operation of a well ordered structure of inquiry. Differences over the fundamental structure of psychoanalysis,[1]* however, will not soon be resolved and, because of this, the following presentation is divided into three parts. This chapter is an outline of the structure, Chapter 3 a more detailed examination of its basic terms, and Chapter 4 an attempt at symbolic representation. Psychoanalysis is here conceived as organized therapeutic inquiry into the experiential field of relatedness and communication. The structure of this inquiry may be demarcated by five orders—observation, definition, transformation, explanation, interpretation. As such, it is that branch of psychology which is designed to clarify the operation of unconscious processes and patterns in personal experience. Its central observations are set off into two clusters of definition—transference, resistance, anxiety which derives from the patient's participation and counteranxiety, counterresistance, countertransference which derives from the psychoanalyst's participation. These two clusters of defined observation, in whatever combination they are described to occur, are then transformed in accordance with three pairs of postulates—genesis and function, structure and dynamism, immediacy or affect and reflection or cognition. These postulate transformations make possible still further observations which are then used to explain

---

distorted, disturbed and difficult aspects of the original observations by the theory of unconscious experience.

All interpretation of unconscious experience depends, however, on the interpreter's—psychoanalyst's or patient's—philosophy of experience and value which, as distinct from empirical and systematic psychology, is interpretive metapsychology. Since the early formulation of instinctual dialectics, various psychoanalysts have constructed several other metapsychologies by which to interpret the meaning of psychological distortion, disturbance and difficulty or even, in the larger view, human life and universal experience—those, for example, of struggle for power, collective unconscious, pure will and so on. No matter which metapsychology a particular psychoanalyst happens to believe and live, of course, his patients are still free to offer personal perspectives which best suit the meaning of their own lived experience. On the other hand, empirical, systematic and interpretive efforts of any one psychoanalyst may be aligned within a structure of inquiry which also characterizes similar efforts of all other psychoanalysts. First, he makes empirical observations to describe certain processes and patterns in the experiential field of therapy. Second, he introduces operational definitions to specify distortions in perception, disturbances in awareness and difficulties in living. Third, he adopts postulates to transform defined observations. Fourth, he applies the theory of unconscious experience to both the original and the transformed observations in order to explain distortion, disturbance and difficulty. And fifth, he proposes one or several metapsychologies to interpret these psychological problems as part of a general philosophy of life.

A. STRUCTURE

The structure of psychoanalytic inquiry may now be outlined as consisting of steps, levels or orders which are empirically and systematically related to one another. These are:

  (1) direct observation of gross experiences,
  (2) operational definition of empirical terms,
  (3) formulation of general postulates,
  (4) integrative theory of explanation, and
  (5) interpretive metaphor or metapsychology.

(1) through (4) outline both the empirical and practical and the
systematic and theoretical in psychoanalytic inquiry, while (5)
represents interpretive and speculative perspectives on this
structure of inquiry. All psychoanalysts carry out the psychoanalytic procedure by virtue of (1) through (4) but, while
they—no more, no less than their patients—also have public and
private perspectives at (5), it is proposed that metapsychologies
neither make nor break the psychoanalytic character of their
psychotherapeutic efforts. The distinction of psychology from
values, in this structure, may be firmly drawn for heuristic purposes between (4) and (5), suggesting both a structural way to
avoid the therapeutic consequences of confusing psychological
with social and moral contexts of experience and a practical
way to avert the dead end of moralistic exercises in psychoanalytic inquiry. Heuristic purposes aside, the problem of
values may be said to have discernible effects, of course, on
every psychoanalytic experience at every step of its ordered
structure of inquiry. But it is being identified as (5), here, in
order to emphasize essential differences between psychology and
values. In no way is this intended to imply, however, that
psychoanalytic patients do not consider judgments of value as
significant as judgments in psychology for self-knowledge. The
intention, here and throughout, is only to stress that these two
sectors of judgment are neither interchangeable nor reducible.

  Comprising empirical and systematic orders of the structure,
(1) through (4) are necessary for the conduct of psychoanalytic
inquiry. While these orders are not sufficient for the experience
of psychoanalytic therapy, it is not for any reason of pure logic
but for the purely factual reason that psychoanalysts and

patients all have philosophies of life, as well, which are in some sense operant in their experiential fields of therapy and which in no sense constitute the structure of their inquiries. From this fact, again, it is possible to draw the clinical line between structure of inquiry and experience of therapy. Only those aspects of (1) which are defined at (2) can then be transformed at (3) and explained at (4). But such other aspects of (1) as the psychoanalyst's or patient's philosophy of experience and value belong to (5), however, because they provide social and moral—that is, metapsychological—contexts in which inquiry gives form to therapy. This clinical line is being drawn, here, in accordance with a special perspective of (5), of course, in which (1) through (4) of this proposed structure are also distinct from (5). This perspective is closely aligned with philosophies which cherish the values of humanism, science and democracy and which may be expected, therefore, to provide metapsychology for experiences of psychoanalytic therapy concerned with the values of individuality, truth and freedom.

Thus, the psychoanalyst attempts to explain certain observable processes and patterns at (1) by bringing them within the scope of an appropriate structure of (2), (3) and (4). He attempts this before, during and after bringing them within the scope of his perspective at (5). The structure of his inquiry may be considered explanatory because it is systematic and intelligible, and scientific because it also remains grounded in empirical observation.[2] The employment of any symbolic notations and mathematical representations is nothing more, however, than a matter of practical convenience.[3] Neither purely symbolic nor purely deductive, then, (4) is closely linked to (2) through the transformational mediation of (3). At the explanatory root of this structure, however, is the use of a psychoanalytic theory without which there is no point to any organized structure. No chain of its deductions is ever coherent or certain enough to demonstrate the actual existence of any process or pattern which does not arise in empirical observation: this derives from the absence of necessary connections among matters of fact.[4] Even the most rigorous of pure deductions which is independent of observable implications, it is clear, does not demonstrate the actual existence of anything in particular.

Conduct of therapy is art, its structure of inquiry is science. The aim of psychoanalysis, as science, is to get at the empirical and systematic foundations of this structure, in order to show how wide varieties of procedure rest upon and evolve from these foundations. Gross experience in the therapeutic field consists of a complex multitude of observable processes and patterns, continually passing into one another unexplored and unknown. They exhibit characteristics and relations which, under appropriate conditions, can be defined as recurrent processes and patterns. When recurrently observed and defined, they suggest transformations and explanations which can be derived from the structure that both follow from and, in turn, make possible additional observations. Such transformations and explanations are not only systematically related to one another but are also empirically rooted in actual therapeutic experience which is open to further inquiry from (1) through (5). Aside from this relation of the systematic to the empirical, it remains a major problem of psychoanalytic inquiry to discover how clinical requirements of its structure are satisfied by observations of its therapeutic effects when, at the same time, there is no sure way of knowing whether selected observations are the most relevant to a particular phase of inquiry or the most significant for later applications of the overall structure. Questions of relevance and significance are best answered at later stages of the total therapeutic inquiry but, even then, it usually is not clear whether the patient requires answers in

order to close his therapeutic experience or looks for them only
to satisfy his psychoanalyst's structural criteria of inquiry.

To consider these questions further, it is worth recalling some
history. The earliest phases of psychoanalysis cannot be discarded as being entirely error, pseudoscience or superstition.
But beyond hypnocathartic therapy and the pressure procedure,
and moving into the present, is the more integrated and refined
phase in which single but solid observations can establish significant results. Sheer repetition of such observations, after
three or five or a dozen are made to eliminate excess and sim-
plify formulation, does not contribute much either to the overall structure, however, or to the solidity of its theory. Since
the early phases, it has become far less relevant for systematic
psychoanalysis than for teaching purposes in seminars and
supervision, to seek corroboration by the mere addition of similar instances. At present, postulates and theory demarcate the
structure of useful psychoanalytic observation in terms of transference, resistance, anxiety and counteranxiety, counterresistance, countertransference. Processes and patterns outside
this structure cannot be so observed as to be defined within it,
and they have no determinate place in the ordered inquiry.
The point is, while such processes and patterns are not ruled
out of the experiential field of therapy, their value is left open
to the interpretation of each individual undergoing psychoanalytic experience.

(1) Gross Experience

There is widespread agreement, no doubt, about the patient's
gross experience in the therapeutic field of inquiry. Regardless
of the type of therapy, there must be some psychological symptoms and syndromes in his gross experience with which a practitioner can begin, some definable distortions, disturbances or
difficulties with which he can work and from which anyone in

any type of therapy, at least by our cultural conventions, expects to be relieved as a result of the collaborative effort. About these presented aspects of gross experience, the psychoanalyst has to make a series of observations. At this first order of psychoanalytic structure,[5] then, is the practically infinite number of observations which can be made in the practically infinite fields of therapy to describe the dominant psychological aspects of distortions in perception, disturbances in awareness, difficulties in living. A psychoanalyst makes his special observations, as well, in accordance with operational definitions he later applies, in order to specify which aspects of which problems he expects to treat psychoanalytically. These observations will be found in statements x_n,[6] below. He proceeds, therefore, to operational definitions which are also called coordinating definitions or rules of correspondence but, for present purposes, these are interchangeable.

(2) *Operational Terms*

In contemporary psychoanalysis, it is well established that the operational terms a psychoanalyst applies to the experience of his patient are transference, resistance, anxiety, which are stated in *t, r, a*. The notion of regression is not considered a second-order term, however, because it lacks the direct observational clarity of transference, resistance, anxiety. To develop the reasons for this view, here, would obviously take us far afield, for they are very extensive.[7] The present chapter is limited to the place of each term in the ordered structure, while the next one is made up of their formulations as well as their relations to one another.

Clinical study of the transfer of experience, distorted and genuine, is Freud's great contribution: He created a general and systematic context of therapeutic inquiry into its particular and empirical psychological processes and patterns. But he never considered it a private discovery or a special possession of his id model—physicians and patients, educators and students among others, he suggested, always knew and appreciated the meaning of its operation. Of course, he also set forth large speculations about its metapsychology, trying to interpret it and all other significant aspects of the human psyche in accordance with his instinctual dialectics. As one result, disagreement among post-Freudians—between, especially, the biological and the cultural Freudians—has turned about the exclusivity and, therefore, about the usefulness of instinctual dialectics. At present, the metapsychologies of psychoanalysis fall into three groups: biological using the id model, modified biological and cultural and interpersonal using the ego or interpersonal model, psychological using the model of shared experience. For all, however, transference is a major operational term.

Resistance is a second operational term. No matter which of the perspectives on metapsychology—biological, ego or interpersonal, psychological—a particular psychoanalyst happens to adopt, all agree to define resistance as any process or pattern which a patient interposes between himself and his emergent insight during therapeutic inquiry.

The third is anxiety, a later addition to the second order. Originally conceived strictly as psychic representation of somatic excitation, there was nothing psychological to be done about its conditions of origin. With the rise of ego or interpersonal psychology, both the origins and the functions of anxiety were opened to direct psychoanalytic exploration. Within the present structure of psychoanalytic inquiry, definitions of transference, resistance, anxiety are entirely psychological: The experiential field in which these processes and patterns are observed and described, the analysis by which they are transformed, explained and interpreted, the goals to which their therapeutic resolution point, are all stated in psychological terms.

Psychoanalytic inquiry is viewed as taking place through time in the experiential field of therapy and, today, this view is probably beyond question. As taking place through time in the experiential field of therapy, of course, it resembles all other types of psychotherapeutic inquiry. But it essentially differs from them in that, involving at least two persons of whom one may be far less real and genuine than distorted and disturbed in the other's perception and awareness, it also builds certain operational terms of the psychoanalyst into its structure of inquiry. These are counteranxiety, which is the psychoanalyst's anxiety in response to his patient, counterresistance which is his resistance and countertransference which is, of course, his transfer of experience—all viewed as taking place through time in a common field of therapy; and they are stated in *ca, cr, ct*. This prefixing of counter to transference, resistance, anxiety is simply to distinguish the study of the patient from that of his psychoanalyst.

As thus far sketched, first-order observation and second-order definition make up the empirical base of psychoanalysis. At this stage of the inquiry, nothing is yet done which a patient can reasonably construe as reconstruction of his distorted self. For he has done little more than review a multitude of observations about his gross experience and, with his psychoanalyst, specify from among them certain processes and patterns for later exploration in this intensive therapeutic inquiry—to transform and explain these defined observations and, then, interpret them.

(3) *Postulates*

To systematize his work, the psychoanalyst now moves on to the third order. The established points of view—genetic, topographical, dynamic, economic, structural—from which some biological Freudians study defined observations belong, properly, to this third order of the structure. They are being called postulates instead, however, because classical points of view are inextricably tied to biological metapsychology and, therefore, are not easily used in the other perspectives. The following selection is based in part on the original points of view, in part on later modifications which were introduced by the ego and interpersonal psychologists, in part on certain aspects of actual psychoanalytic inquiry which are now being fitted into the structure. Required above all, however, is a choice set of postulates whose fate as scientific psychology is not directly tied to the fate of any single perspective on metapsychology. When applied to the study of defined observation in great varieties of cases over long periods of time, some hardly change, some are soon reconstructed, some need careful revision, some do not prove useful. A good example of a well established postulate is, in classical terms, the genetic point of view—about which serious disagreement is practically nonexistent. A good example of a reconstructed postulate is, again in classical terms, the topographical point of view—in which unconscious first referred to an area rather than a quality of processes and patterns in relation to one another. A good example of a revised postulate is, still in classical terms, the economic point of view—with the notion of quantity but a metaphor about such felt experience whose transformations are as well done by the postulate of reflection. On the other hand, recent attempts to add the adaptive point of view to the classical set of postulates has dubious psychological value because it is not directly relevant to the empirical and systematic orders but to a special philosophy of experience which is rightfully at the order of interpretive metapsychology. In these instances, then, basic postulates of psychoanalytic structure are retained and reconstructed, revised and restricted as they undergo extended testing and critical examination.

By far the oldest and most widely accepted postulate is history or genesis, and it is stated in G. One psychoanalytic way to treat defined observations of the first and second orders is, accordingly, from a historical point of view. It governs the search for genetic sources of a particular relatedness and communication, whether first observed and defined as transference, resistance or anxiety, which the patient brings to the experiential field of therapy. When defined observations of counteranxiety, counterresistance, countertransference are being explored, it may be necessary to apply this postulate as well as each of the others, however, in very special ways—which not only depends on a particular psychoanalyst's personal style of relatedness and communication but, of course, may also hold equally true for their application to the patient's experience. A major advantage of mapping this structure of inquiry, it may already be clear, is to outline the general limits and possibilities of psychoanalysis, as distinct from its use in a particular experience of therapy.

The next postulate by which to transform defined observations is function, and it is stated in F. It answers the question of how various psychological processes and patterns relate to one another and to other components of the ongoing psychoanalytic experience in which they appear.

The third, stated in S, is structure. Although this postulate resembles the classical structural point of view, it is now possible to discover where in the organization of personality which underdeveloped and unintegrated process or pattern tends to persist, and do so with a pluralistic perspective on metapsychology.

The fourth is dynamism, which is stated in D. Again, the classical dynamic point of view is here modified in regard to biological theory of personality development, for the increase and decrease of instinctual energies alone are hardly adequate for judging everything a patient does to put transference, resistance or anxiety into operation. Rather, this postulate is now extended to include satisfaction of needs, realization of goals and fulfillment of ideals, and treat general strivings in relation to needs, goals and ideals, as these strivings can be observed and defined under psychological conditions.

The fifth postulate is immediacy. As stated in I, it is being proposed in order to facilitate exploration of affective, non-cognitive or irrational aspects of the experiential field of psychoanalytic therapy. And the last one, reflection, is stated in R. It is being proposed in order to facilitate exploration of cognitive, mediating or rational aspects of that experiential field. Immediacy refers to affective or irrational experience, to the development of direct feeling, to the noncognitive and immediately presentational; reflection refers to cognitive or rational experience, to the development of logical intelligence, to the mediative and representational. If the processes and patterns of affect and impulse, of cognition, logic and intelligence—of, even, the Freudian ego's directive and autonomous functions—are to have a place and a point in psychoanalytic inquiry, they require such postulates as immediacy and reflection in the conduct of psychoanalytic therapy. Among the reasons, then, for proposing these two new postulates are, first, to align psychoanalytic structure with basic traits of human experience and, second, to account for the very existence of psychoanalytic activity itself.

(4) *Theory*

With these six postulates which transform the originally defined observations, the psychoanalyst has not yet realized his inquiry. Thus far, he has participated in the emergence of an experiential field of therapy, or working therapeutic alliance, which supports the promise and hope and faith in a useful psychoanalytic outcome. He has made a set of empirical observations, specified certain of them by an operational definition and transformed these defined observations by the given postulates. But he has yet to apply the theory of unconscious experience, which is stated in U. All psychoanalysts use it to explain discrepancies between original observations and those which result from postulate transformations and, in this way, explain distortions in perception, disturbances in awareness, difficulties in living. This is the basic theory of psychoanalytic structure, for both the rationale of inquiry and the explanation of results, and its steady application through the whole structure distinguishes psychoanalysis from other psychotherapies. It is with this theory in view that third-order postulates are selected, as their main purpose is to expedite its application to the results of inquiry at the first and second orders. When the theory of unconscious experience does apply to defined and transformed observation, it explains the persistence of distortions, disturbances and difficulties in personal psychology to the extent, at most, that psychoanalysis is capable of explaining them within the limits of these first four orders of inquiry. The most important thing a psychoanalyst can do, then, is apply his distinctive theory to defined and transformed observations in the experiential field of therapy. In this way, he joins first-order observation and second-order definition, the two empirical orders, to third-order postulation and fourth-order explanation, the two systematic orders.

(5) *Metapsychologies*

After empirical and systematic inquiry, of course, belong the wide varieties of metapsychology which have been constructed to interpret human experience and its problems. These are stated in $[M_n]$. There have always been and, rightfully, still are many deep and heated disagreements over these interpretive metapsychologies because they are, essentially, speculative. They involve philosophies of experience and theories of value and are interpretations of life, about which large differences persist among practicing psychoanalysts. Metapsychology may be said to have the same relationship to psychology, in this structure of psychoanalysis, as any metascience has to its science. Whatever else it is or does, it contains the most general interpretation of the most pervasive traits of its subject matter. Under this heading are, of course, all interpretive and speculative metapsychologies from instinctual dialectics, struggle for power, collective unconscious and pure will to the various humanisms which are now current. It is hard to know whether their exponents would in each case agree with this ordering of psychoanalytic structure or with their placement among metapsychologies at the fifth order. It goes without saying, however, that new metapsychologies may always be added to this structure, and that all five orders are open to future enlargement and modification.

B. INQUIRY

Recall, now, the patient's gross experience in which are intertwined his distortions in perception, disturbances in awareness, difficulties in living. When the psychoanalyst begins to work toward describing and specifying them for further inquiry, an experiential field of therapy comes into being. For psychoanalysis to take place, now, the patient must continue to seek its experience of therapy and, of course, the psychoanalyst must continue to apply its structure of inquiry—irrespective, in any case, of their commitment to established metapsychologies. This therapeutic field is made up of both the patient's and the psychoanalyst's whole range of experience and, obviously, includes the psychoanalyst's perspective on metapsychology. But, it is necessary to add, the patient's perspective is not excluded from this therapeutic field because, no less than his psycho-analyst, he also has a philosophy of life—perhaps not as self-consciously organized as his psychoanalyst's, yet this is not al-ways the case. At one time or another, most psychoanalysts probably work with patients from whom they learn a good deal about psychological problems and even more, from the unusual patient, about philosophies of life. It is not excessive to assert, in any case, that the psychoanalytic patient has reached a level of personal experience which, in effect, manifests elements of a philosophy of life. Though the elements are usually private and, in the seriously disturbed, far too primitive and under-developed for systematic purposes, they have significant fea-tures, nonetheless, which are ordinarily associated with psycho-analytic philosophies of experience. Every man—and this, in-deed, is the point—has some such philosophy in or around the experiental field of therapy.

As soon, then, as the patient begins to present his psycho-analyst with distortion, disturbance or difficulty which they can define psychologically, an experiential field of therapy exists. But the patient's problem has to be jointly defined and it has to be understood as such by both participants. For if the patient cannot present a problem, or if the psychoanalyst cannot see one, there is nothing to work with. The real hurdle, here, is to determine why the patient seeks psychological therapy, and why that particular psychoanalyst decides to attempt it with him. All this is, generally speaking, part of every structure of therapeutic inquiry. If therapy succeeds, resolution of the psychological problem is relevant to its own special structure of inquiry. This approach is general enough to include most experiential fields of therapy and specific enough, as well, to focus most psychological problems and most psychotherapeutic procedures. Most important of all, however, it underlines structures of inquiry as distinguishing the several psychotherapies from one another, and experiential field of therapy as the most general matrix in which structured inquires take place. When, for example, the resolution is psychoanalytic experience, it may be considered a direct result of introducing psychoanalytic structure into the experiential field of therapy. It may be assumed, of course, that no matter what a psychotherapist may think he is doing with a patient, he is always attempting to introduce one or another structure of psychological inquiry. When, on the other hand, nondirective structure is introduced into the experiential field of therapy, its result is neither hypnotic nor psychoanalytic, of course, but nondirective experience. This, to be sure, is self-evident. It may also be assumed, then, that no matter what a psychotherapist may think he is doing with a patient, he is always attempting to introduce one or another structure of psychological inquiry, whether his structure happens to be among the established types or, as a highly individualistic one, is not yet formulated. But what may not be self-evident and, therefore, may be worth emphasizing is, first, that structure of inquiry governs the possible experience of therapy and, second, that the structure adopted sets both the terms and conditions of the results achieved.

If this outline of psychoanalytic structure is applicable and fruitful, the step to symbolic representation is relatively easy—so much so that, at the present stage of knowledge, it may be well worth considering how useful it is to move in this direction.[8] What follows, nevertheless, is a rudimentary scheme of symbolic representation. First and second are the empirical, third and fourth are the systematic orders of inquiry, and every psychoanalyst works with them regardless of his metapsychology at the fifth order. Observations of transference are symbolically represented as t_n because its possible varieties and nuances are, after all, infinite. This also holds true, of course, for symbolic representations of resistance as r_n, anxiety as a_n, counteranxiety as ca_n, counterresistance as cr_n, countertransference as ct_n. Once these observations are specified, their definitions may be represented as t, r, a and ca, cr, ct. These defined observations may be transformed in accordance with the postulates of genesis, represented as G, function as F, structure as S, dynamism as D, immediacy as I, reflection as R. Defined and transformed observations are explained by the theory of unconscious experience, represented as U, and they may then be interpreted by perspectives on metapsychology, best represented as $[M_n]$ because of the plural and even discordant philosophies and values to which psychoanalysts variously adapt their empirical and systematic results. Note that observations are in small letters, regular type, and that definitions are in small letters, italicized; postulates are in capital letters, regular type, and theory is in capital letters, italicized; interpretive symbols are in capitals, regular type and bracketed.

An illustration may now best develop relations among empirical and systematic orders of psychoanalytic inquiry, leaving preferences in fifth-order interpretation to the particular psychoanalyst, the particular patient and their particular conditions of shared experience. In this structure, there are six ways to study processes and patterns which are transferred and countertransferred, resisted and counterresisted, anxious and counteranxious. These are the third-order postulates or systematic points of viewing and transforming defined observations of the first and second orders. Although the following illustration is being simplified for discursive illustration, its transformations suggest that postulates belong in three pairs. Genesis and function in statements G and F depict the temporal dimension both in history and communication and in development and relatedness; structure and dynamism in statements S and D depict the patterns of striving and the organization of needs, goals and ideals; immediacy and reflection in statements I and R depict the affective and cognitive aspects of experience. When the inquiry is fully done, any one postulate transformation may be considered compatible with any other, but presentation of more than one set of results at a time is too complex and cumbersome for discursive analysis. In each postulate transformation, therefore, its relations to the others are suggested but not explicitly worked out.[9]

A single defined observation of transference is to be illustrated. Its postulate transformations apply with equal validity to other observations of transference in statement t_n, resistance, anxiety in statements r_n, a_n, as well as counteranxiety, counterresistance, countertransference in statements ca_n, cr_n, ct_n. Although observations of the psychoanalyst are not regularly studied, any comprehensive outline of psychoanalytic structure extends, of course, to include them. After demonstrating over the years that transference, resistance, anxiety, as defined in statements t, r, a, can open the patient's experience to intensive inquiry, it is appropriate to enlarge the therapeutic field to include counteranxiety, counterresistance, countertransference, as defined in statements ca, cr, ct, if only because of the observable consistency of all psychological proccesses and patterns, no matter whose they are and, in respect to the integrity of every human psyche, no matter whose it is. There is no a priori reason for theory or practice, furthermore, to make this set of psychological terms unrelated and inapplicable to the psychoanalyst when, in fact, it has already been related and successfully applied to the patient. Beyond consistency of psychic process and pattern as well as consistency in actual practice, it is also possible to derive the operation of the psychoanalyst's terms from the patient's by using clusters of definition. Just as transference may be observed, that is, in response to both resistance and anxiety, resistance in response to both transference and anxiety, and anxiety in response to both transference and resistance, so transference, resistance, anxiety may be observed in individual or collective response to counteranxiety, counter-resistance, countertransference—each, in turn, observed in individual or collective response. But in all psychoanalytic therapy, the main result of introducing third-order postulates is, however, to structure the application of fourth-order theory of unconscious experience to the distortion, disturbance or difficulty which the patient orginally presents for intensive inquiry.

Consider, now, the orders of definition, postulation and explanation which are based, of course, on observation and description of gross experience. The example is:

t_1 The patient expresses an unreasoning dislike of the psychoanalyst.

In order to appear in this form, of course, statement t_1 already contains the results of many psychological and logical transformations. These transformations are not exclusively derived from the psychoanalytic structure, however, but also from the logical structure of thought and the syntactic structure of language.[10] But turning, now, to a patient's expression of unreasoning dislike, it provides for observation in many direct and indirect ways. He may find fault with his psychoanalyst's tie, furniture or location of office, he may criticize his personal habits, social sense or worldly understanding, or he may reject his feelings, thoughts or attitudes. For such reasons as these, he may express himself in terms which range from mild annoyance and condescension through irritation and distaste to contempt and sheer hatred. In order to define such feelings, thoughts and attitudes, no matter their specific content, the psychoanalyst moves his structure of inquiry to the second order which specifies particular aspects of unitary patterns—here, as transferred—to the extent that they can be studied in psychoanalysis. After establishing for his patient and himself the transferential character of this expression of unreasoning dislike, he may state its definition:

t   When the patient introduces a significant change of re-
               latedness and communication, verbal or otherwise, about
               his psychoanalyst, transference may be observed to be pres-
               ent, leaving to further exploration and analysis its genuine
               and distorted features.

By specifying statement t_1 by statement t, the psychoanalyst applies an operational definition to a particular communication of his patient. Thus far, he adds nothing concrete or useful to the patient's understanding of his original problem but, by doing this, he has in fact begun to describe its empirical linkage to the structure of psychoanalytic inquiry. Beyond this, however, he adds nothing to a defined observation which is now waiting to be transformed by third-order postuates. Ordinarily, postulate transformations are not carried out in terms of any special sequence or fixed arrangement but, rather, in accordance with workable themes of the particular therapeutic field. These themes are set by such factors as the patient's interests and awareness, his psychoanalyst's concerns and awareness, the availability of collateral information where and when the observation is defined as an observation of transference. In this illustration, however, all six possibilities follow in order to trace the transformational range of the third order. First consider:

G   Historical and developmental aspects of psychological
               processes and patterns are subsumed under the postulate of
               genesis. They provide the basis for understanding both
               the rise of processes and the development of current pat-
               terns in various fields of experience and through various
               stages of growth.

By coordinating statements t_1 and t with statement G, the psychoanalyst applies the postulate of genesis to a defined observation of transference. If this succeeds, it directs clinical attention to inquiry into both history and development so that the patient may explore other experiences in which he has undergone a similar unreasoning dislike of persons other than the psychoanalyst—early, middle and late childhood, pre-adolescence, early, middle and late adolescence, and even adulthood. Under this postulate, no a priori value is attributed to historical information uncovered in one period of development as distinct from that which is uncovered in any other, while the attempt to locate firm historical origins of this unreasoning dislike in the patient's experience, as he focuses the attempt directly on his own past, remains the primary objective of this postulate transformation. But genetic analysis of transference, if successful, still is psychoanalytically incomplete. Thus far, an observable attitude of unreasoning dislike is defined as transference and transformed to reveal its significant historical and developmental aspects. In order to use this information, however, for completing the systematic side of psychoanalytic structure, which is done to explain and resolve aspects of the original problem by the conscious reintegration of certain processes and patterns that previously operated beyond awareness, it is necessary to invoke theory at the fourth order, which is:

U Psychoanalytic inquiry enlarges the scope of awareness of psychological information which clarifies problems in living. This information spans the repressed, distorted and unrealized processes and patterns of past, present and future experience, and is used to reintegrate those in with those outside awareness.

In so far as psychoanalytic inquiry is governed by this theory of unconscious experience, it is capable of delineating forgotten and repressed information, expanding the scope of awareness and bringing this new information to bear on problems in living. Above all, this inquiry seeks to apply statement U to the results of transforming statements t_1 and t, here, in accordance with statement G. The explanatory power of statement U does not derive from the fact that, in each case, forgotten and repressed material invariably results from applying statement G, for such material does not always result from genetic analysis. Its explanatory power derives, rather, from the fact that in no case can the genetic postulate have psychoanalytic significance, whatever it may be said to have in other structures of psychotherapeutic inquiry, without the theory of unconscious experience to guide reintegration in awareness of forgotten and repressed history and development. The particular psychoanalyst who also believes on grounds other than this genetic transformation, however, that the patient is forgetting and repressing instinctual dialectics, struggle for power, collective unconscious, pure will and so on, which are given primary interpretive roles in $[M_n]$ has introduced fifth-order speculation about his use of statement U to guide his transformation by statement G of statements t_1 and t.

For a rounded analysis of this clinical illustration, it is necessary to review the postulates of function, structure, dynamism, immediacy and reflection. This will not prove too tedious, it is hoped, for the student of psychoanalysis who would sketch the special outcome of each postulate transformation[11]; others may turn directly to Chapter 3, page 77. Consider, now, the postulate of function, a complement to that of genesis, which is:

F   The action and reaction of processes or patterns, as these produce a nexus with others within the experiential field in which they appear, are studied by the postulate of function. It characterizes both the relatedness and the communication of processes and patterns.

By coordinating statements t_1 and t with statement F, the psychoanalyst applies the postulate of function to a defined observation of transference. If this succeeds, it directs clinical attention to inquiry into both communication and relatedness so that the patient may explore special phases of the therapeutic field in which he experiences this attitude of unreasoning dislike, to study its antecedent processes and patterns, his and his psychoanalyst's, which converge to become its context—something either participant may have felt, said or done to evoke this specific form of communication and relatedness. The operant conditions under which this unreasoning dislike is transferred onto the psychoanalyst deserve study in their own right and outside the therapeutic field, as well, in order to determine how far this transfer is generalized. Under this postulate, no a priori value is attributed to functional information uncovered in one set of conditions as distinct from that which is uncovered in any other, while the attempt to identify the functions of the patient's unreasoning dislike in the therapeutic field, even if he focuses primarily on extratherapeutic experience, remains the objective of this postulate transformation. But functional analysis of transference, if successful, still is psychoanalytically incomplete. Thus far, an observable attitude of unreasoning dislike is defined as transference and transformed to reveal its functional aspects of communication and relatedness. In order to use this information, however, for completing the systematic side of psychoanalytic structure, which is done to explain and resolve the original problem by conscious reintegration of certain processes and patterns that previously operated beyond awareness, it is again necessary to invoke statement U. In so far as psychoanalytic inquiry is governed by this theory of unconscious experience, it is capable of delineating parataxic and disjunctive information, expanding the scope of awareness and bringing this new information to bear on problems in living. Above all, this inquiry seeks to apply statement U to the results of transforming statements t_1 and t, here, in accordance with statement F. The explanatory power of statement U does not derive from the fact that, in each case, parataxic and disjunctive material invariably results from applying statement F, for such material does not always result from functional analysis. Its explanatory power derives, rather, from the fact that in no case can the functional postulate have psychoanalytic significance, whatever it may be said to have in other structures of psychotherapeutic inquiry, without the theory of unconscious experience to guide reintegration in awareness of parataxic and disjunctive communication and relatedness. The particular psychoanalyst who also believes on grounds other than this functional transformation, however, that the patient is communicating parataxically and relating disjunctively because of $[M_n]$, which states a perspective on metapsychology, has introduced fifth-order speculation about his use of statement U to guide his transformation by statement G of statements t_1 and t.

The postulate of structure is:

S   Structure is described in terms of constituent processes and patterns, integrative contexts of inquiry, fields of experience or human situations. This postulate denotes the meaningfully organized aspects of connected and mutually dependent psychological processes and patterns.

By coordinating statements t_1 and t with statement S, the psychoanalyst applies the postulate of structure to a defined observation of transference. If this succeeds, it directs clinical attention to inquiry into both the pattern and the organization of experience so that the patient may explore the formative relation of this attitude of unreasoning dislike to other similar and dissimilar attitudes—to understand where in his organization of attitudes it is located, about which personal conditions in his development it is patterned, and how it acquires operational form in the therapeutic field. Under this postulate, no a priori value is attributed to structural information uncovered in one set of conditions as distinct from that which is uncovered in any other, while the attempt to identify the patient's pattern of unreasoning dislike in the organization of his personality remains the primary objective of this postulate transformation. But structural analysis of transference, if successful, still is psychoanalytically incomplete. Thus far, an observable attitude of unreasoning dislike is defined as transference and transformed to reveal its structural aspects of pattern and organization. In order to use this information, however, for completing the systematic side of psychoanalytic structure, which is done to explain and resolve the original problem by conscious reintegration of certain processes and patterns that previously operated beyond awareness, it is again necessary to invoke statement U. In so far as psychoanalytic inquiry is governed by this theory of unconscious experience, it is capable of delineating underdeveloped and unintegrated information, expanding the scope of awareness and bringing this new information to bear on problems in living. Above all, this inquiry seeks to apply statement U to the results of transforming statements t_1 and t, here, in accordance with statement S. The explanatory power of statement U does not derive from the fact that, in each case, underdeveloped and unintegrated material invariably results from applying statement S, for such material does not always result from structural analysis. Its explanatory power derives, rather, from the fact that in no case can the structural postulate have psychoanalytic significance, whatever it may be said to have in other structures of psychotherapeutic inquiry, without the theory of unconscious experience to guide reintegration in awareness of underdeveloped and unintegrated pattern and organization. The particular psychoanalyst who also believes on grounds other than this structural transformation, however, that the patient's patterns are underdeveloped and his organization is unintegrated because of $[M_n]$, which states a perspective on metapsychology, has introduced a fifth-order speculation about his use of statement U to guide his transformation by statement S of statements t_1 and t.

Consider, now, the postulate of dynamism, a complement to that of structure, which is:

D   Dynamism embraces any psychological reason why par-
           ticular processes or patterns modify the direction of ex-
           perience toward satisfaction of needs, realization of goals
           and fulfillment of ideals. It studies that psychological
           striving which subtends the means-ends continuum.

By coordinating statements t_1 and t with statement D, the psychoanalyst applies the postulate of dynamism to a defined observation of transference. If this succeeds, it directs clinical attention to inquiry into strivings so that the patient may explore frustrated needs, failed goals and unfulfilled ideals which emerge during his therapy. Although his dislike is unreasoning, it may nonetheless express a personal striving which deserves to be explored in its own right, in terms of genuine and distorted relations to his psychoanalyst as well as others in his past and present outside the therapeutic field. Under this postulate, no a priori value is attributed to dynamic information uncovered in one set of conditions as distinct from that which is uncovered in any other, while the attempt to identify dynamisms of the patient's unreasoning dislike in his therapeutic experience of striving for needs, goals and ideals remains the primary objective of this postulate transformation. But dynamic analysis of transference, if successful, still is psychoanalytically incomplete. Thus far, an observable attitude of unreasoning dislike is defined as transference and transformed to reveal its dynamic strivings for needs, goals and ideals. In order to use this information, however, for completing the systematic side of psychoanalytic structure, which is done to explain and resolve the original problem by conscious reintegration of certain processes and patterns that previously operated beyond awareness, it is again necessary to invoke statement U. In so far as psychoanalytic inquiry is governed by this theory of unconscious experience, it is capable of delineating frustrated, failed and unfulfilled information, expanding the scope of awareness and bringing this new information to bear on problems in living. Above all, this inquiry seeks to apply statement U to the results of transforming statements t_1 and t, here, in accordance with statement D. The explanatory power of statement U does not derive from the fact that, in each case, frustrated, failed and unfulfilled material invariably results from applying statement D, for such material does not always result from dynamic analysis. Its explanatory power derives, rather, from the fact that in no case can the dynamic postulate have psychoanalytic significance, whatever it may be said to have in other structures of psychotherapeutic inquiry, without the theory of unconscious experience to guide reintegration in awareness of frustrated needs, failed goals and unfulfilled ideals. The particular psychoanalyst who also believes on grounds other than this dynamic transformation, however, that the patient's needs are not satisfied, goals not realized and ideals not attained because of $[M_n]$, which states a perspective in metapsychology, has introduced fifth-order speculation about his use of statement U to guide his transformation by statement D of statement t_1 and t.

Both the fifth and the sixth postulates are being proposed to provide a base in psychoanalytic structure for the conditions of learning experience and the terms of self-directed change. The postulate of immediacy is:

I   Directly presented affect, unrehearsed and noncognitive impulse and both qualitative and unanalyzable aspects of

psychological contexts of process and pattern are treated by
the postulate of immediacy. Immediate affect and impulse
provide the integrating thread during inquiry for closure,
synthesis and consummatory experience.

By coordinating statements t_1 and t with statement I, the psychoanalyst applies the postulate of immediacy to a defined observation of transference. If this succeeds, it directs clinical attention to inquiry into affect and impulse as definable and irreducible, or distorted and incongruous, and into the immediate
context of felt experience in which this attitude of unreasoning
dislike is encountered. Although dislike is patently negative,
since it is being felt as unreasoning or irrational, the patient
may yet become aware of both positive and negative affect and
impulse which accompany its unreasoning quality, especially to
distinguish immediatism of defensive phenomenology from
immediacy of genuine and irreducibly personal experience.
Under this postulate, no a priori value is attributed to information about immediate experience uncovered in one set of conditions as distinct from that which is uncovered in any other,
while the attempt to determine whether the dislike is genuine
and irreducible and the unreasoning qualities distorted and
incongrous, or the unreasoning qualities are genuine and irreducible and the dislike distorted and incongruous, or both
the attitude and its qualities are either genuine and irreducible or distorted and incongrous, remains the primary objective of this postulate transformation. But immediate analysis
of transference, if successful, still is psychoanalytically incomplete. Thus far, an observable attitude of unreasoning dislike
is defined as transference and transformed to reveal its immediate aspects of affect and impulse. In order to use this information, however, for completing the systematic side of psychoanalytic structure, which is done to explain and resolve the
original problem by conscious reintegration of certain processes

and patterns that previously operated beyond awareness, it is again necessary to invoke statement U. In so far as psychoanalytic inquiry is governed by this theory of unconscious experience, it is capable of delineating distorted and incongruous information, expanding the scope of awareness and bringing this new information to bear on problems in living. Above all, this inquiry seeks to apply statement U to the results of transforming statements t_1 and t, here, in accordance with statement I. The explanatory power of statement U does not derive from the fact that, in each case, distorted and incongruous material invariably results from applying statement I, for such material does not always result from analysis of the immediate aspects of experience. Its explanatory power derives, rather, from the fact that in no case can the postulate of immediacy have psychoanalytic significance, whatever it may be said to have in other structures of psychotherapeutic inquiry, without the theory of unconscious experience to guide reintegration in awareness of distorted affects and incongrous impulses. The particular psychoanalyst who also believes on grounds other than this immediate transformation, however, that the patient's affects and impulses are distorted and incongruous because of $[M_n]$, which states a perspective on metapsychology, has introduced fifth-order speculation about his use of statement U to guide his transformation by statement I of statements t_1 and t.

Consider, finally, the postulate of reflection, a complement to that of immediacy, which is:

R   Indirect and representational thought, rehearsed and cognitive inference and both mediating and analyzable aspects of psychological processes and patterns are treated by the postulate of reflection. It focuses on logical and rational aspects of the experience of therapy.

Because of skittish views of reason and reflective intelligence in recent psychoanalytic discussion—best understood, perhaps, as

frustrated reactions to the obduracy of intellectualized defenses—the postulation of reason and reflective intelligence as
a systematic point of view has been avoided. This results in a
structure of psychoanalytic inquiry that, strangely enough, does
not possess the tools by which to construct even itself—but
which, in the experience of psychoanalytic therapy, also puts
the patient in the ambiguous position of both using his head in
private and protecting his psychoanalyst against doubts about
the validity of a structure which lacks this point of view or
postulate to guide the exercise and study of cognitive operations.
By coordinating statements t_1 and t with statement R, the psychoanalyst applies the postulate of reflection to a defined observation of transference. If this succeeds, it directs clinical attention
to inquiry into the logic of this attitude of unreasoning dislike
so that the patient may check it for rational documentation
and objective reference, to determine where and when his
process of thinking missed the mark. Not infrequently, failure
of reflective analysis is due to distortion of immediate experience, and when one changes the other also changes. But the
decision has to be made empirically in each case since, no less
frequently, failure of reflective analysis can be traced to blind-
spots due to inexperience or unawareness. Under this postulate,
no a priori value is attributed to information about reflective
aspects of experience uncovered in one set of conditions as distinct from that which is uncovered in any other, while the attempt to identify reflective activity in the attitude of unreasoning dislike remains the primary objective of this postulate transformation. But reflective analysis of transference, if successful,
still is psychoanalytically incomplete. Thus far, an observable
attitude of unreasoning dislike is defined as transference and
transformed to reveal its reflective aspects of observation and
inference. In order to use this information, however, for
completing the systematic side of psychoanalytic structure,

which is done to explain and resolve the original problem by conscious reintegration of certain processes and patterns that previously operated beyond awareness, it is again necessary to invoke statement U. In so far as psychoanalytic inquiry is governed by this theory of unconscious experience, it is capable of delineating irrational and illogical information, expanding the scope of awareness and bringing this new information to bear on problems in living. Above all, this inquiry seeks to apply statement U to the results of transforming statements t_1 and t, here, in accordance with statement R. The explanatory power of statement U does not derive from the fact that, in each case, irrational and illogical material invariably results from applying statement R, for such material does not always result from reflective analysis. Its explanatory power derives, rather, from the fact that in no case can the reflective postulate have psychoanalytic significance, whatever it may be said to have in other structures of psychotherapeutic inquiry, without the theory of unconscious experience to guide reintegration in awareness of irrational observations and illogical inferences. The particular psychoanalyst who also believes on grounds other than this reflective transformation, however, that the patient's observations and inferences are irrational and illogical because of $[M_n]$, which states a perspective on metapsychology, has introduced fifth-order speculation about his use of statement U to guide his transformation by statement R of statements t_1 and t.

Within the structure of psychoanalytic inquiry, then, the above illustration shows how to derive a psychoanalytic fact through observation, definition, transformation and explanation. In addition to these empirical and systematic orders, however, there is the interpretive order and its several speculative visions in $[M_n]$. But no one is necessarily or exclusively tied to this structure. Essentially philosophies of experience and theories of value, each in its own way accounts for the existence and meaning of this fact of transference which is observed in statement t_1, defined in statement t, transformed in statements G and F, S and D, I and R and explained in statement U. Despite the common factual core of all psychoanalytic inquiries from the first through the fourth orders, since the fifth order has no uniform perspective on metapsychology, its use in the structure does not entail uniform results.

Chapter 3

Structure of Inquiry II

ANY FREE SCIENCE needs the courage of empirical observation and the right to systematic reconstruction. When psychoanalysis no longer combines continuity of inquiry with freedom to change, it will disintegrate as science and become history of science. What it now requires, in the formal view, is a structure of inquiry which can be demarcated by direct observation, operational definition, postulate transformation, explanatory theory and interpretive metapsychology. This view makes it possible to distinguish both empirical and systematic orders more sharply from the interpretive and speculative order of all three models of clinical psychoanalysis. While it hardly resolves every difficulty and inconsistency of the past, it does point in two useful directions—to a firm structure already in existence and to the still unexplored and unmapped frontiers. Progress in psychoanalytic inquiry thus far has mainly resulted from the empirical derivation and systematic transformation of operational terms. With wide agreement about transference, resistance, anxiety and counteranxiety, counterresistance, countertransference, it also is necessary to follow a set of simple yet general postulates which, together, make useful and effective the explanatory theory of unconscious experience. Beginning with personal communications of gross experience, as illustrated in Chapter 2, the inquiry moves from definitions of operational terms to the postulates which, though not directly testable and independently confirmable, are best warranted by their demonstrated relations to operational definitions; for, like a bridge, they coordinate defined observations with each other and, by transforming them, with explanatory theory. In this way, they also expand the empirical field, generating hunches and clues, inferences and hypotheses which then hint and suggest, guide and govern new observation of gross experience.

This structure of psychoanalysis is being developed essentially to define the range and scope of a special type of psychological therapy. The structure itself is not the same, however, as actual procedure of therapy: It governs and guides special phases of actual procedure. Its observations, definitions, postulates and theory are never found in a pure state; they are generally found embedded in a complex of factors—intrapersonal and interpersonal, transpersonal and nonpersonal—which both psychoanalyst and patient bring to their common effort at therapeutic inquiry. In other words, application of the structure is to be confirmed by extended investigation. Potentially, everything either co-participant ever experiences of his self, family, culture and society may be encountered in the therapeutic field, while distinctive features of their common effort, in so far as these are psychoanalytic, are its logical derivatives. Hence, organic symptoms and disease, although observed in particular psychoanalytic inquiries, are not directly studied by this structure; their study belongs to biochemistry and neurophysiology. Definition and adoption of social roles, although clearly observed as well, are not strictly within its scope either; these belong to sociology and social psychology. Judgments of value, although observed as well, also are not strictly within its scope; these belong to ethics and moral philosophy. Nor are cultural attitudes and philosophies of experience, while observed, its special domain; their study belongs to anthropology and metaphysics. This structure of inquiry, it is proposed, governs the conduct of a therapy which is psychoanalytic, and distinctly so, by virtue of its special empirical observations and definitions and by virtue of special systematic postulates and theory.

The existence of this situation has long been well known, namely that psychoanalysis intersects with such other fields as biochemistry and neurophysiology, sociology and social psychology, ethics and moral philosophy, anthropology and metaphysics, yet it still needs further clarification. These many intersections, for example, do not constitute mergers. From the fact that it is often difficult to relate psychoanalysis to these various fields of inquiry, it is not necessary to infer that such relations are therefore nonexistent or indefinable. Nor is it necessary to conclude, for any known and legitimate reason, that they ever can be so defined as to mask the field of psychoanalysis from awareness, replacing its structure of inquiry and duplicating its experience of therapy. It is from the steady and focused study of human psyche, and not soma, culture or society, that the working structure of psychoanalysis has gradually evolved. Neither as necessary nor as desirable consequence, on the other hand, is organism severed from environment, psyche separated from soma, individual isolated from society, or human split from culture. These consequences and their variations derive from perspectives which are not, themselves, psychological; they derive from special interpretations and speculations which are, instead, perspectives on metapsychology. The integrity of psychoanalytic structure need in no way be violated, therefore, by its assimilation to competing theories of value and even incompatible philosophies of experience. Sad and hard though it may be to acknowledge, psychoanalysis offers no singular revelation about the true, the good or the eternal—despite the many such revelations which, indeed, have been seriously suggested—and its findings often are easily appropriated for good or ill by competing and even incompatible ideologies of its environing culture.

Again consider, here, that psychoanalytic structure is not the same as psychoanalytic experience. Even though psychoanalysis

shares certain of its general postulates with all other psychotherapies, the use of this whole structure distinguishes psychoanalytic from other psychotherapeutic experiences. From a
procedural point of view, the ways this structure is effective in
any one psychoanalytic experience, however, usually differs
very significantly from the ways it is effective in every other.
No two psychoanalysts realize it in precisely the same way, and
no psychoanalyst can realize it in precisely the same way, even,
with any two patients. This qualification has to be stressed,
of course, to accommodate the personal uniqueness of each
participant in the inquiry. There is nothing mysterious about
this: It merely extends into psychoanalysis the distinction of
theoretical from practical, general from particular, essential
from accidental. And there is nothing mysterious about its
meaning and use: It provides for a central structure by which to
organize myriad varieties of psychoanalytic experience and in
which to differentiate empirical and systematic from interpretive orders of this evolving field of inquiry. Whether in the
particular case a psychoanalyst considers it valuable to report
personal history, for example, or countertransference dreams
to his patient is not a theoretical issue; it is, among other things,
a matter of individual decision, an outgrowth of personal style,
a special phase of a particular shared experience. But whether,
in practice, he deals openly with countertransference and with
its relations both to counteranxiety, counterresistance and to
transference, resistance, anxiety as operational definitions of
psychoanalytic structure, however, actually affects the structure
of his therapeutic inquiry. And once again, the point is, despite
the many personal variations which psychoanalysts may adopt
to work through variable experiences with individual patients,
their inquiry has a general structure by which they practice in
common.

Do psychoanalyst and patient have to agree in detail about
any single philosophy of experience or theory of value, then, in

order to realize this structure? According to some, such overall agreement speaks well for the outcome of inquiry as therapeutic experience while, according to others, it may well obscure the unconscious roots of irrational dependency and unstable individuality which extend through the transactions of both participants and distort their shared experience. Beyond these divergent opinions, however, stands the enduring fact of psychoanalysis—despite, even, the brevity of its history—whose structure has been organized from the therapeutic inquiry of many particular psychoanalysts who published their differences in metapsychology and many particular patients who did not publish theirs. Similiarities and differences among Freud, Adler, Jung and Rank for example, are articulated in detail and defended by these metapsychologists and their followers, but similarities and differences among Anna O. who originated the talking cure, Emmy von N. who hit upon the method of free association, Dora who first enacted a well defined transference resistance, and many other patients whose contributions remain anonymous, as well as their agreements and disagreements with their psychoanalysts's metapsychologies, are no longer recoverable. A history of psychoanalytic structure, to the extent that its development is recorded in the literature, would probably detail the contributions of known participants in psychoanalytic inquiry. But it also would probably show, moreover, that metapsychology is not the distinctive feature of this inquiry since, on the one hand, any rounded perspective on experience and value is compatible with all structures of psychotherapy and, on the other, all serious philosophers of experience are also serious metapsychologists without ever practicing psychoanalytic therapy or even formulating their perspectives in response to any actual experience of therapy.

Certain particular features of psychoanalytic experience vary from therapeutic field to therapeutic field and, therefore, set each one off from the others. By virtue of being psychoanalytic, however, these experiences also share certain general features which set them off from the experiences of other psychotherapies. These general features, of course, define the structure of psychoanalytic inquiry, while the particular ones define variable experiences of psychoanalytic therapy. Again, in this respect, structure of inquiry is not the same as experience of therapy. The postulate of genesis, for example, belongs to a limited number adopted at the third order for the coordination of psychoanalytic inquiry while, in practice, actual appeal to psychological history depends upon concrete conditions of the particular psychoanalytic experience. At the third order, this postulate is a general feature of the structure while, in actual therapy, its use is a very specific matter of ongoing experience. To illustrate this point in still another way: Relations among second-order definitions are general features of the structure which can be derived by postulate transformation, yet the discovery of which process or pattern of transference at any point makes a particular patient anxious is always made in a particular field of therapy.

In this view, it is also possible to distinguish psychoanalytic from other aspects of a therapeutic experience and, then, to outline the psychoanalytic aspects by a special structure of inquiry. It is not reeducation of the patient or transvaluation of his values but theory of unconscious experience which governs its application to psychological therapy. This view therefore indicates how, first, the structure of psychoanalysis is set within an experiential field of therapy, second, only selected aspects of psychotherapeutic experience are intensively studied in accordance with this structure and, third, the experience of psychoanalytic therapy is only partly devoted to structured orders of psychoanalytic inquiry. In other words, some psychoanalysts may focus on reeducation or transvaluation and unself-consciously realize these five structured orders, others may focus directly on this special structure of inquiry and leave reeducation and transvaluation to the patient's own synthesis of his therapeutic experience, but none can practice psychoanalysis without applying this special structure. It is probably clear, by now, that this special structure is being here conceived as an empirical, systematic and interpretive outline by which psychoanalysts may guide their conduct of inquiry in the practically countless experiences of therapy.

It is probably also becoming clear, however, that this notion of structure of inquiry, together with its distinction from experience of therapy, directs further attention to a whole nest of neglected issues. To put this into sharper focus, compare structure of inquiry with an actual structure of, for example, a building. The structure obviously is not the building, since a building's purpose determines choice of materials to complete it, selection of appliances to equip it and arrangement of furnishings to make it habitable. It is no less obvious that, in order to exist, a structure need not be fully, partly or at all completed, equipped or furnished, that in no meaningful sense does a building even exist without a structure or that any number of buildings may have a similar structure even though those for private use do not outwardly resemble those for public and commercial use, To drop the analogy: It is theoretically wrong to consider empirical and systematic orders invalid or non-operational because the structure itself cannot be applied in all respects to every particular case. It is practically wrong, as well, to believe a priori that this structure cannot acquire empirical support in a systematic way because there are countless particular psychoanalysts, countless particular patients and countless therapeutic experiences—from those beginning with the gross experience of therapy and working toward the realization of psychoanalytic structure, to those concentrating on this special structure and leaving the psychoanalytic experience to a patient's working through it himself.

Metapsychologically, all psychoanalytic structure is part of the experience of psychoanalytic therapy, and all psychoanalytic experience is part of the experiential field of therapy. This can be illustrated in the Figure 1. *A* is psychoanalytic structure, *B* psychoanalytic experience and *C* field of therapy. Every seasoned psychoanalyst gets the pace and measure of his

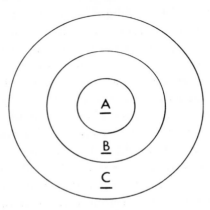

Figure 1.

own procedure, moving from *A* through *B* to *C* or the other way around, or starting from any one at random and working through the other two. He practices a highly specialized procedure which, of course, is structured by *A*, interpreted by the larger yet more particular B, and finally applied to the still larger yet far more particular *C*. In other words, he may productively limit his active participation to the rationale of *A*, participate in the self-reconstructive phases of *B* as he is so inclined by his own metapsychology or his patient's active invitation but, then, leave to the patient all uses of psychoanalytic knowledge and personal insight for the particular needs, goals and ideals of his therapeutic experiences in *C*.

Structurally, of course, all psychoanalysts seek to realize A in every case, some are able to realize it only in selected cases, and a few may well do it without having very much direct psychoanalytic interest. This can be illustrated in Figure 2. Note, here, that A intersects with B, that B intersects with C, but that no one fully coincides with the other two. Following the diagram of Figure 2, it is likely that some phases of every psychoanalytic experience are in no significant sense structure

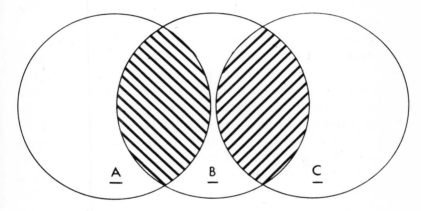

Figure 2,

of inquiry or experience of therapy, even though they are still part of the experiential field. They need have no significant relation, even, to the empirical or systematic orders of inquiry which both psychoanalyst and patient may judge desirable and realizable. Only select phases of psychoanalytic experience are derived from psychoanalytic structure and directly integrated within the experiential field of therapy. Although some phases of A are also B and, through B, may eventually touch C, others of A are, however, neither B nor C, just as some of B are neither A nor C, and just as some of C are neither A nor B. That is, some aspects of psychoanalytic structure are not directly related to psychoanalytic experience or field of therapy, some aspects of psychoanalytic experience are not directly related to psycho-analytic structure or field of therapy, some aspects of field of therapy are not directly related to psychoanalytic experience or psychoanalytic structure. Some examples are: in psychoanalytic structure, replacement of the economic point of view by other third-order postulates; in psychoanalytic experience, a patient's decision to marry; in field of therapy, environmental change such as buying a new house—in each case, the event may be directly related to its own sphere without necessarily affecting the other two.

In accordance with Figure 2, moreover, it is probable that the transcript of a terminated analysis could be fitted to A, B and C. There are collaborative efforts at psychoanalytic inquiry which do not all succeed, as in A minus B; there are personal efforts at integrating therapeutic results during a psycho-analytic experience which is also occupied with many matters other than psychoanalytic structure or hard realities of daily life, as in B minus A plus B minus C; and finally, there are many incidents and experiences which are part of the field of therapy without also being related, however, to actual probabil-ities of psychoanalytic therapy, as in C minus B. This proposed research is not being attempted, here, because it requires a mi-nute review of clinical transcripts and is out of keeping with the organization of this study. If the overall approach proves illuminating, however, as even so brief a consideration of Fig-ures 1 and 2 suggests it should, then there is no need at this point to undertake a transcript analysis. Both Figures 1 and 2, in any case, make it possible to visualize relations of psycho-analytic structure, or A, to field of therapy, or C, through the medium of psychoanalytic experience, or B, in which these relations are in fact actualized. The two diagrams are intro-duced, then, mainly to depict some relations among these three spheres. Illustrative rather than exhaustive, they also show

how it is possible to demarcate psychoanalytic structure as a distinct topic of study without, moreover, separating it from such related topics as experience of therapy and field of therapy. And they make it possible, finally, to show how this structure is but one among many which are designed for psychological inquiry into the field of therapy—short-term, nondirective, hypnotic and so on, each of which yields its own type of experience when it is introduced into the therapeutic field, from short-term to nondirective, to hypnotic and so on.

A. SCIENCE

Not unlike other psychologies, psychoanalysis is intimately related to evolving approaches to the human psyche. These approaches are open to the procedures and results of all fields of science but, for psychoanalytic inquiry, they have to be reworked in essentially psychological terms in order to express the empirical and systematic relations of this but no other structure of inquiry. All definitions, postulates and theory are formulated, therefore, to set forth the psychoanalytic structure of any therapeutic effort as distinct from the psychoanalytic experience of any result. From a historical point of view, these orders of inquiry have undergone modification in theory and practice, yet psychoanalysis did not come into its own until their application succeeded in the therapeutic field—some at the center and others at the periphery, some earlier and others later, some in rudimentary and others in mature form. But no history of psychoanalysis can replace a formulation of its logical structure—so that questions about when a definition, postulate or theory first appeared and how it was then stated, what processes and patterns it first covered and how it results were then evaluated, can be clearly distinguished from questions about the best statement and application of that definition, postulate or theory which are now available. The continuing significance of psychoanalytic structure derives, therefore, from its continuing modification and enlargement in psychological terms to fit evolving approaches to the human psyche as studied in the experiential field of therapy. The best way to define psychoanalytic facts, at present, is by means of psychoanalytic structure, and the best way to demarcate this structure, in turn, is still by means of these same facts—which does not, of course, preclude the possible unions of psychoanalysis, at the order of interpretive metapsychology, with perspectives of other psychologies and other human sciences. But no psychoanalyst deals effectively with his patient's communications and no patient deals effectively with his psychoanalyst's communications, however, in terms and under conditions other than those which are made available and reliable by the empirical and systematic structure that both participants use to guide their common efforts at psychoanalytic therapy.

One further point about these evolving approaches to the human psyche: In psychoanalytic structure, these approaches are not treated as universal judgments about the basic composition of human nature or, even, as tentative guides to the statement of definitions, postulates and theory. Hardly the exclusive property of psychoanalysis, they are also adapted to perspectives in other psychotherapies and other sciences of the human psyche. But it is misleading to attempt a whole appropriation of these perspectives and results without, at the very least, a simple reconstruction of them for use in psychoanalytic inquiry. When reconstruction fails, the appropriated perspectives and results give rise to distortion and choke off further development all around. The best example of this, to date, is the often declared yet still unrealized union of psychoanalysis with biochemistry and neurophysiology in such loose and weak amalgams as neuropsychiatry, psychosomatic medicine and biogenetic psychodynamics which, thus far of necessity, block rather than coordinate fields of inquiry. Another more recent example of this is, of course, the still loose and rather weak amalgam of psychocomputer analysis which attempts to formulate significant clinical investigation in mathematico-experimental terms and whose structure of inquiry, thus far of necessity, is far more behavioral than psychological. It is not necessary, however, to treat these various efforts as entirely misleading and misguided, but it is not yet possible to consider them contributions to the advancement of psychoanalytic inquiry and therapy. Their answers are still in the future.

May psychoanalysis, meanwhile, be called science? This question, at present, may be given a qualified yes. When, sixty and seventy years ago, a small cadre of Viennese researchers were at work in comparative isolation, neither the question nor the answer was relevant. These pioneers did not stop long enough to ask it of their rapidly expanding field of inquiry, let alone answer it to the critical satisfaction of scientists and philosophers who were then on the sidelines. Simply and courageously, they just assumed they were engaged in constructing a new science, using the best patterns of inquiry which were then both usable and productive in the study of live experience of psychological problems. As they published their results, however, curiosity about this new psychology began to grow. At about the same time, academic psychologists and philosophers of science began to focus critical tools on every aspect of classical psychoanalysis, and they found it wanting in respect to the empirical verifiability of its results and the explanatory power of its metapsychologies. Significantly, however, they used standards of criticism which had been developed in structures of physical and chemical science, laboratory methods of experiment and mathematical analysis. And they worked over the structure of psychoanalysis like a scientific stepchild, expecting it to justify itself in accordance with

standards and structures which did not, themselves, derive from
direct clinical studies of human experience, its processes and
patterns, problems and reconstructions. As a result, they placed
psychoanalysis beyond the scientific pale. Although man is
not to be treated as an object or thing, they rightly contended,
the structure and results of studying his live experience, however, still have to abide by the best theory of inquiry now being
used in the general analysis of knowledge. Every psychoanalyst
who is concerned about his empirical and systematic orders of
inquiry, of course, would readily agree with this contention.
Yet, in response to it, some are also ready to take psychoanalysis
out of relation to science altogether—some into absurdist
philosophies and theologies, others into eastern and western
varieties of mysticism. But another alternative is open, as
well. When, on the basis of such fields of inquiry as physics
and chemistry, it can be asserted that psychoanalysis is no
science, then it may be noted that its subject matter is live experience which qualitatively differentiates it from these other
fields of inquiry. The implications directly follow: either that
a structure of inquiry be patterned at a level which is broad
and general enough to include psychoanalysis among scientific
inquiries, or that clear distinctions be formulated among the
major sciences to make room for psychoanalysis as independent
and self-corrective inquiry. Awaiting further clarification of
this issue, psychoanalysts may be reasonably content to continue
working at their structure of inquiry and, meanwhile, leave the
more general decision to philosophers of their science.

It is mainly because study of the scientific status of psychoanalysis belongs to the philosophy of science, then, and not to
the psychoanalysis of distorted, disturbed and difficult experience that this question now has to be answered with but a
qualified yes. With varying degrees of success, past psychoanalytic inquiries have established a structure of observation,

definition, transformation, explanation and interpretation, which is conditioned by both its subject matter and its actual procedures and which is designed to realize empirical and systematic orders that are at once applicable, reliable, open to change. Between a current generalization in the philosophy of science, however, and a working structure which yields the best psychoanalytic inquiry known, since neither is under pressure to confirm any absolutisms, the choice need not be arbitrary. So, yes, psychoanalysis is science; and no, it does not satisfy all criteria which ordinarily secure the factual validity of theory in other sciences. Basic changes in the overall perspective obviously have to be attempted both from philosophy of science and from psychoanalysis. The effort to demarcate a structure of psychoanalytic inquiry originates, in part, as awareness of this problem. If it meets the antecedent requirements of either discipline or both, this is not the only factor in judging its value, since success here depends far more on the avenues of investigation it opens up than the antecendent questions it finally lays to rest. But if it fails to meet them, this too is not the only factor in judging its value, since they may both be, in fact, narrow empirically and defective systematically. For while there are, indeed, certain philosophic refinements of observation, definition, transformation and explanation which every psychoanalytic structure must eventually realize, there is still the hard empiricism of any actual psychoanalytic inquiry with which all philosophy of science must inevitably come to terms.

In this connection, consider the most generic meaning of science, finally, that of knowledge. All knowledge may be called science without, it is clear, having the organizational structure of any single science—like that, for example, of mathematical physics. Since the limits and possibilities of a subject matter set the conditions and terms of its own structure of inquiry, no single subject matter need set the standard structure for all scientific inquiries. And this is true for psychoanalysis no less than, say, physics or chemistry. Whether one structure of inquiry can ever be so broadly formulated that it covers all fields of science, from mathematical physics all the way to psychoanalysis of experience, remains a central issue for philosophy. But no such general structure can ever be so narrowly formulated as to ostracize the substance of any one science, and then make its claim stick on a priori grounds. Psychoanalysis may rest its case, for the present, on its power to study certain observable clusters of psychological process and pattern by means of appropriate definitions, postulates and theory at various orders of inquiry, and on its power to apply this empirical and systematic study to the resolution of certain psychological problems of gross experience. This, indeed, has been the controlling aim of psychoanalysis from its early beginnings in hypnocathartic therapy—deriving its definitions from the observation of distorted, disturbed and difficult experience, formulating its postulates to govern the transformation of such defined observation, and refining its theory to account for the explanatory range of defined and transformed observations which extend into unconscious experience. In pursuit of this aim, there is greatest agreement about the two sets of definition, transference, resistance, anxiety and counteranxiety, counterresistance, countertransference, about the formulation of select postulates which pair off as genesis and function, structure and dynamism, immediacy and reflection, and about the theory of unconscious experience. Widespread and seemingly interminable, however, are differences over metapsychology which color general statements of psychoanalysis by admixtures of philosophy of experience and which base speculative attempts at programmatic theories of value, preferred codes of behavior or mystical quests for salvation on the special findings of psychoanalytic inquiry.

(1) *Observation*

Direct phenomenology of gross experience is so complex that, without systematic simplification, no structure can be organized for psychoanalytic inquiry. While the defect of direct phenomenology is hopeless complexity, and the risk of structured inquiry is useless oversimplification, the choice between defect and risk is, clearly, to demarcate the most adequate structure of inquiry possible. The problem of observation is probably most slippery and at the same time, however, most crucial in the use of psychoanalytic structure. It is the problem, briefly, of defining the special facts of this therapy as distinct from those of other therapies, and as distinct from varieties of interpretive metapsychology which are speculated to relate psychoanalytic facts to, for example, general and social psychology, physics and chemistry, sociology and economics, anthropology and religion, philosophies of experience and theories of value. A clinical structure of psychoanalytic inquiry, it is proposed, can best deal with this problem. Some would do it, instead, by making controlled experiments with psychoanalytic results under laboratory conditions—even, at times, with animals—or by submitting these results to psycho-computer analyses. Others would treat the psychoanalyst as a therapeutic machine which is designed to control human behavior and whose immediate responsibility it is to shape a patient's personal psychology to his environment of social and moral values. And still others would turn absurdist and mystical in the extreme belief that rational and durable answers to this problem of observation are no longer possible. These departures from the actual psychoanalytic experience may be understood, perhaps, as disheartened responses to the defects and failures of past efforts to demarcate a structure of psychoanalytic inquiry. From the fact that these efforts still leave much to be desired, however, radical departures from psycho-analytic inquiry do not, of course, necessarily follow. Even though this structure is not yet adequately described, if only because some psychoanalyses already have been more or less successfully completed, it may at least be said in some sense to exist.

Nor does it follow from the great and varied difficulties with this problem of observation, furthermore, that no further at-tempts can be made to resolve it. There is still the old and true path of all personal psychologies to be reconsidered in new ways. Critically, to be sure, but on faith supported by empirical discovery, this path leads back through the history of psychoanalysis and, before that, to the hypnotherapeutic work of Bernheim, Breuer and Charcot. It is the path of natural observation—that of directly working with live fields of related-ness and communication in which a structure of inquiry may be applied to recurrent patterns of process—without commit-ment to any reductive naturalisms, of course, but simply as an obvious reference to direct observation of live experience. It seems a bit strange, now, to uphold this view of observation as natural in contrast, perhaps, to mathematico-experimental and psychocomputer analyses or absurdist and mystical philos-ophies which are considered unnatural and, in some curious sense, therefore more capable of producing reliable knowledge about human experience. Such standards as precision, sim-plicity, accuracy and reliability are the reasons most frequently given for abandoning natural observation. But if, to satisfy these standards, actual therapeutic inquiry is no longer the operational source and testing ground of psychoanalytic ob-servation, definition, postulation and theory, then it is the standards themselves which have to give way. An unfortunate alternative, otherwise, is to deny that psychoanalysis is scientific inquiry—which, indeed, reflects the very narrow view of first proposing a single uniform structure of science and then excluding all nonconformist inquiry from it. The more fruitful alternative is to derive standards of psychoanalysis from problems and results of its own field of inquiry. For these standards require careful screening and formulation so that, in actual therapeutic inquiry, they sustain the live character of processes and patterns which are observed and described, defined and transformed, explained and interpreted.

Why this flight, then, from the experiential field of therapy? The problem of observation is so complex that it is practically impossible to select a set of fixed criteria which invariably produce the experience of psychoanalytic therapy. This does not simply result from the fact that mind and experience are no longer reduced to fit mechanical categories which can then be independently manipulated and transformed. Even when a classical id therapy adopts the mechanistic theory of mind and, with its reductive categories, supports analyses of neurotic and psychotic experience, it still does not break down the problem of observation into simple relations of cause and effect, or describe these relations as strict co-variations of independent and dependent variables under strictly controlled conditions. From this mechanistic tradition in scientific thought, of course, stems the misleading psychoanalytic supposition that once a variable process or pattern is labelled, it has to continue so labelled in future reference for the rest of that inquiry. But even a quick glance at the purpose of psychoanalytic therapy would suggest, however, that this supposition is, in fact, contrary to fact. Decisive for the intensive effort at psychoanalysis is the quest for secure knowledge about unconscious experience which, in some sense, is unexpected, unprecedented and even unpredictable in conscious contexts of daily experience. Like a beating pulse, this steady quest for new guidelines to reconstruction of the distorted self is an underlying feature of all intensive psychoanalytic effort. Aside from this misleading aspect of mechanistic thought, however, it is no simple matter to describe the sort of observation which may be directly structured as psychoanalytic in the experiential field of therapy. There are intercurrent ambiguities and uncertainties of psychoanalytic observation which, in any case, are ineluctable—arising, as they do, from the historical changing and dynamic searching of psychological movement; and at one time or another, every seasoned practitioner encounters them. After beginning a psychoanalytic procedure, he may encounter unplanned social contingencies and moral dilemmas, for example, whose analysis and disposition cannot be effectively limited to their psychological constituents. After beginning a supportive procedure, he may find himself in the middle of a serious yet unplanned psychoanalytic inquiry or, from the other side, even begin a psychoanalysis and then, in accordance with unexpected and unpredictable information, have to modify or replace it with another psychotherapy. While in training for psychoanalysis, the student therapist benefits, of course, from experience with varieties of procedure with a wide range of psychological conditions—the wider the better—but in gaining this experience, he also learns to identify empirical and systematic differences among the various procedures and their respective observations. And if he would modify procedures and objectives to suit changing fields of therapy, it becomes all the more important for him to identify which features are and are not distinctive of psychoanalytic inquiry.

Again note, here, that since most problems presented for therapy usually are very complex, they also possess factors which extend beyond psychoanalysis and into society and culture, politics and morals, religion and philosophy. These factors seem to suggest, paradoxically, that psychoanalysis cannot be practiced as strictly psychological therapy because it cannot

be exclusively concerned about distorted, disturbed and difficult aspects of experience. The paradox, however, is only apparent. By convention, structure of inquiry may be restricted
to observations and definitions of transference, resistance, anxiety and counteranxiety, counterresistance, countertransference,
to postulate transformations of genesis and function, structure
and dynamism, immediacy and reflection, and to theory of
unconscious experience—while it is the experience of therapy
which may be said to involve society and culture, politics and
morals, religion and philosophy. Two reasons for general
agreement on this convention are immediately evident. First,
naturally, are the many sorts of problematic communication
which, in their original form and content, have no direct relevance to the psychoanalytic structure. When a patient seeks
advice or instruction, for example, about some incidental event
in his daily life, even the psychoanalyst who observes and defines this as transference, resistance, anxiety and, from a metapsychological point of view, also considers it nonpsychoanalytic
to respond at all, may still find it impossible to avoid responding
in a human way. Although not best qualified, he may engage
in educational activity which is beyond his competence—stimulated, perhaps, by unresolved counteranxiety, counterresistance, countertransference, caught up in the live human com-
pulsion to respond to his co-participant, or encouraged that
engagement in direct educational activity at one point increases
later probabilities of successful inquiry. As long as he is not
unconsciously pressured, however, to ignore both fact and
consequence of his activity in the immediate and cumulative
development of therapy, this nonpsychoanalytic intervention
may hamper but does not preclude future efforts which are
warranted by later observation. The fact that his work no
longer is, as it never could be, absolutely pure psychoanalysis
does not mean, of course, that it no longer is at all, and never

again would become, psychoanalytic. No such purity is possible in observation, definition, transformation, explanation and interpretation of live experience, and this leads to the second reason why the psychoanalyst cannot be exclusively concerned with psychological aspects of experience. He cannot carry out his procedure in strict abstinence because his patient, interested in reconstructing his distorted self, needs to become especially aware of his self-reconstructive capabilities which are repressed together with the repressed roots of his self-distortion. If the psychoanalyst were directly to supply a patient, however, with the psychological conditions and resources to do it, he would have to consider continuing in this nonpsychoanalytic role until his patient developed new patterns to function autonomously, until he resolved a specific problem and terminated therapy only to return when other such problems arose or, even, until the patient died.

For these by no means exhaustive reasons, psychoanalysis is viewed as taking place within an experiential field of therapy.[1*] This view of it, in turn, underlines the importance of a structure of inquiry in which some but, clearly, not all clinical observations become psychoanalytic constituents of that structure. Since all sorts of things human are observed in any field of psychotherapy—anything of human interest, indeed, which is felt and perceived, thought and imagined—the psychoanalyst bases reliability of psychoanalytic experiences on a structure of inquiry which is distinct from short-term, nondirective, hypnotic and other structures and from, of course, the social and moral exchanges of daily life. Observation during psychoanalytic inquiry, therefore, is most relevant to the empirical foundations of its structure. No more than a serial order can be formulated at present, however, to demarcate the clinical

---

* For Notes to this Chapter, see pages 205-206.

structure in which constituent observations are then defined and transformed, explained and interpreted. In relation to this ordered structure alone does psychological observation become psychoanalytic, for only after the first order of observation is linked to the second order of definition can it yield defined observations of the structure.[2] Without proceeding, of course, from the empirical to the systematic—from, in other words, first and second orders of observation and definition to third and fourth orders of transformation and explanation—there is no psychoanalytic observation of fact.

In the first order, then, are gross observations of distorted, disturbed and difficult experience. These are processes and patterns of feeling, thought and attitude which the patient relates and communicates to his psychoanalyst in order to institute a field of psychological study. Not just any feelings, thoughts and attitudes, it is clear, ordinarily become facts of psychoanalytic inquiry. For many are related and communicated in the everyday work of therapy which need have no direct bearing on either the structure or the experience of psychoanalysis. This is not to say they have no intrinsic value for other psychotherapeutic and, perhaps, nonpsychological purposes, and as long as their significance is unknown and underived, there is no clear value to ascribe to them. But it does mean that they are neither definable in psychoanalytic structure nor useful as psychoanalytic experience. Even the so-called free associations, when they truly exist, are not psychoanalytic until they are defined in terms of the second order. Free associations, that is, and direct observations acquire psychoanalytic significance as they are fitted to these operational terms. A patient's expression of affective attitude about his psychoanalyst, for example, may be defined and assigned to the operation of transference. Or his expression of discomfort in word, gesture or body movement, which takes place along a continuum from vague apprehension to sheer terror, may be assigned to the operation of anxiety. Since it is not just any of his communications which are significant in psychoanalytic experience, they are not all equally relevant to psychoanalytic structure. At this level of inquiry, false starts interfere with the reliable definition of observed processes and patterns, yet frequent recurrence of false starts may then involve the use of still other definitions such as resistance or counterresistance. What, then, are psychoanalytic facts? More than brute phenomena and less than indubitable truths, they connote something done or made in the study of live experience to identify processes and patterns of relatedness and communication which can at least be specified for further inquiry by means of the definitions that are now central to psychoanalysis.

(2) *Definition*

In the second order are operational definitions of empirical terms. These, together with first-order observations, make the empirical foundations of psychoanalytic inquiry. The line between the two is drawn very thin to emphasize the mutually corrective relation of observation and definition. A crucial product of this relation, in developing psychoanalytic inquiry, is the gradual enlargement of the definition of transference from the oedipal nucleus of childhood to processes and patterns of personal psychology which derive from earlier and later experience in or outside the immediate family. Closely tied to this, of course, is the gradual refinement of its definition from being just irrational and distorted to being both irrational and distorted and rational and genuine, depending on how it is capable of being explored and analyzed during detailed inquiry. In this way, operational definitions are developed and reworked, for their statement guides actual procedures by which empirical observations of the structure can be made.

Definitions of psychoanalysis, it is proposed, fall into the two natural clusters of transference, resistance, anxiety and counteranxiety, counterresistance, countertransference, and each one denotes three definable types of observation which either participant may suffer and undergo, relate and communicate, in ways that are central to the construction of psychoanalytic inquiry. They are stated in that sequence. The definition of transference is:

t   When the patient introduces a significant change of relatedness and communication, verbal or otherwise, about his psychoanalyst, transference may be observed to be present, leaving to further exploration and analysis its genuine and distorted features.

Recall, here, that the notation *t* represents the definition of transference at the second order of inquiry. Also note, again, that symbols used to represent empirical orders are in small letters—observations in regular type and definitions in italics; symbols used to represent systematic orders are in capital letters —postulates in regular type and theory in italics; and symbols used to represent the interpretive order are capitals, regular type and bracketed.[3] And note, as well, that since transference and countertransference, together, provide useful parameters of the psychoanalytic field of inquiry, the one is first, the other is last. The definition of resistance is:

r   When, as a function of specific manifestations of transference, the patient relates and communicates derivative processes and patterns which oppose continued collaboration on the problem at hand, these functional derivatives are named resistance.

While transference and resistance—as well as anxiety and counteranxiety, counterresistance, countertransference, which are soon to be defined—need not be solely distorted, the notion of distortion is solely a function of all six definitions in structured inquiry. This consideration is based on the likelihood that either patient or psychoanalyst may select from his funded experience a process or pattern of relatedness and communication which yields a genuine and rational perception of his co-participant's personality just as well as he may select one that yields a distorted and irrational perception of him. The definition of anxiety is:

a   When the patient undergoes processes and patterns along a continuum from vague discomfort to sheer terror which accompanies a disruption of collaborative endeavor on the problem at hand, subsequent changes in relatedness and communication may be said to arise from anxiety.

As encountered and studied in psychoanalytic inquiry, anxiety is a mode of response which signals the felt absence of integrative activity. It is viewed as disintegrative for feeling, thought and attitude, on the assumption that an exploratory analysis of its experiential conditions can produce greater clarity of feeling, thought and attitude. The definition of counteranxiety is:

ca   When the psychoanalyst undergoes processes and patterns along a continuum from vague discomfort to sheer terror which accompanies a disruption of collaborative endeavor on the problem at hand, subsequent changes in relatedness and communication may be said to arise from counteranxiety.

The definition of counterresistance is:

cr   When, as a function of specific manifestations of countertransference, the psychoanalyst relates and communicates derivative processes and patterns which oppose continued collaboration on the problem at hand, these functional derivatives are named counterresistance.

The definition of countertransference is:

ct   When the psychoanalyst introduces a significant change of relatedness and communication, verbal or otherwise, about his patient, countertransference may be observed to be present, leaving to further exploration and analysis its genuine and distorted features.

The comments about statements t, r, a also apply to statements ca, cr, ct. About both clusters of definition, however, it may be said that their statement is far more precise than their practical usage can ever be with first-order observations of gross experience. In every ongoing therapeutic inquiry, any two particular co-participants require varying degrees of precision and tolerate varying degrees of ambiguity, of course, as simple matters of personal history, preference and style. While these personal qualities are in no sense deducible from psychoanalytic structure, they usually are decisive when, in a particular field, it has to be known whether certain definitions of gross experience suffice for the maintenance of inquiry, or others need to be introduced for intensification of the inquiry. In spite of these natural limitations, the distinction of observation from definition is both useful and unavoidable,[4] however, in the practice of psychoanalysis; it establishes a procedural context of significance for observations of structured inquiry. But this point will be further clarified when the first two orders are related to the third and fourth. The purpose of constructing second-order definitions is, meanwhile, to single out initial and coordinate conditions so that, from statement t to statement ct, the phrase "in psychoanalysis" is tactily assumed as the inquiry and experience in which these definitions hold. Before involvement in a particular case, of course, it is not possible to state which processes or patterns are significant for the resolution of which problems that are going to dominate that particular therapeutic effort, but it is possible to state definitions such that they adequately circumscribe the empirical range of exploration which both participants undertake in their effort to make it psychoanalytic.

Consider, now, some clinical examples of both clusters of definition. They are for illustrative purposes only and are

simply being listed without reference to the psychoanalytic experience in which they occur. In this study, continuous clinical material is unwieldly because its many dimensions have to
be treated individually and discursively even though they
simultaneously occur in one and the same experiential field of
therapy and, of course, because all of them are not equally
relevant to the structure of psychoanalytic inquiry. Continuous
material, moreover, best illustrates the making of a psychoanalytic experience and, elsewhere,[5] it is presented in accordance with this structure of inquiry. Defined observations of
transference are:

t_1[6]   The patient expresses an unreasoning dislike of his
          psychoanalyst.

t_2 The patient expresses excessive liking for the psycho-
          analyst, regards his as the best or only possible psycho-
          analyst for him, and asserts that no other could assume and
          successfully carry out the therapeutic task.

t_3 The patient is preoccupied with his psychoanalyst to an
          unusual degree between sessions, and imagines remarks,
          questions or situations involving the psychoanalyst. In the
          patient's dreams, the psychoanalyst may appear as himself.

Defined observations of resistance are:

r_1 When the psychoanalyst comments or questions in order
          to hear more information about a particular feeling,
          thought or attitude, the patient tends to ignore its point
          while seeming to respond, and quickly moves to another
          topic.

r_2 The patient finds it difficult to focus on any serious as-
          pect of his problems. He is vague about them, and may dis-
          cuss them as though he were consulting the psychoanalyst
          about his case as one professional colleague to another. He
          may even become drowsy or drop off into light sleep.

r_3 The patient is habitually late for his sessions, or shows
          such other disturbances about time arrangements as not
          wanting to leave or running over the end of sessions. Any

problem about practical arrangements, once mutually agreed and entered upon, belongs to this category.

Defined observations of anxiety are:

a_1 The patient dreads the sessions with his psychoanalyst, and is continually uncomfortable during them.

a_2 The patient seeks to elicit a particularly unpleasant emotional response from his psychoanalyst by provocative remarks, double-edged questions and dramatized or falsified situations.

a_3 The patient undergoes an observable physical change which is unexpected yet characteristic—facial expression, voice pitch, uncontrolled body movements or speech rate. In some unclear and still unexplored way, this change is related to a problem at hand; it sustains continuity of relatedness and communication at points where rational feeling or discursive thought is unavailable.

Defined observations of counteranxiety are:

ca_1 The psychoanalyst dreads the sessions with his patient, and is continually uncomfortable during them.

ca_2 The psychoanalyst seeks to elicit a particularly unpleasant emotional response from his patient by provocative remarks, double-edged questions and dramatized or falsified situations.

ca_3 The psychoanalyst undergoes an observable physical change which is unexpected yet characteristic—facial expression, voice pitch, uncontrolled body movement or speech rate. In some unclear and still unexplored way, this change is related to a problem at hand; it sustains continuity of relatedness and communication at points where rational feeling or discursive thought is unavailable.

Defined observations of counterresistance are:

cr_1 When the patient responds to comments or questions in order to develop information about a particular feeling, thought or attitude, the psychoanalyst tends to ignore its point while seeming to understand, and quickly moves to to another topic.

cr_2 The psychoanalyst finds it difficult to focus on any serious aspect of his patient's problems. He is vague about them, and may discuss them during the session as though his patient were a professional colleague. He may even become drowsy or drop off into light sleep.

cr_3 The psychoanalyst is habitually late for the sessions, or shows such other disturbances about time arrangements as running over the end of sessions, rescheduling a patient with excessive frequency, or finding it impossible to do so with inflexible rigidity.

Defined observations of countertransference are:

ct_1 The psychoanalyst expresses an unreasoning dislike of his patient.

ct_2 The psychoanalyst expresses excessive liking for the patient, regards him as his very best patient, and asserts that no other could assume and successfully carry out the therapeutic task.

ct_3 The psychoanalyst is preoccupied with his patient to an unusual degree between sessions, and imagines remarks, questions or situations involving the patient. In the psychoanalyst's dreams, the patient may appear as himself.

For the sake of simplicity, the defined observations of transference, resistance, anxiety are selected because they can be interchanged with those of counteranxiety, counterresistance, countertransference. No more is implied by this interchange, however, than that psychoanalyst and patient tend to emerge in similar ways as persons and co-participants in the inquiry. In addition to historical usage, moreover, discursive and systematic analysis requires two clusters of empirical terms for their respective co-participation. In a previous study,[7] the axiom of bipolar or reciprocal relations was suggested at the third order to account for this special feature of defined observations of transference and countertransference, resistance and counter-resistance, anxiety and counteranxiety. The difference between the patient's and the psychoanalyst's set of definitions, according to this axiom, does not reside in either the structure or the function of psychological processes and patterns but, rather, in the identity of their possessor. This view of their difference is still valid, of course, but the axiom may be expanded into a formulation to cover and analyze far more complex observation with greater clarity and refinement. In place of this axiom are three pairs of postulates: genesis and function, structure and dynamism, immediacy and reflection.[8] For the axiom does not yield the degree of specificity, furthermore, for transformations of defined observation which are supported by these six postulates. At any event, finally, the statement of fourth-order theory is general enough to be coordinated with all six third-order postulates, yet is not so narrow as to preclude any therapeutic inquiry with whose second-order definitions it can be said that direct observations at the first order have a bipolar and reciprocal relationship.[9]

During actual inquiry, operational definitions are not applied to isolated observations of detachable processes or patterns. Their application depends, above all, on the whole structure, and the making of defined observations therefore has varying outcomes in various experiential fields of therapy. If, as in statements t_1 and ct_1, psychoanalyst and patient express an unreasoning dislike for one another at the outset, therapeutic inquiry most likely terminates then and there. If these attitudes are expressed during later phases of the work, they interlock in ways which prove either mutually enlightening and facilitative or mutually defeating and disruptive.[10] And if they emerge in the closing phases, one or both co-participants may transform t_1 or ct_1 on a reflectively aware basis into a reasoned dislike of specific processes and patterns of the other.

A word about regression: It is not being included among

definitions of the second order since, first, when direct observation can be firmly described as withdrawal from the ongoing context of inquiry, it may as well be treated by the definitions of transference, resistance, anxiety in combination with the definitions of counteranxiety, counterresistance, countertransference and, second, when observations of regression are combined with those of progression to signify backward and forward movements of experience, they may as well be treated in terms of the established postulates of genesis and function, structure and dynamism, immediacy and reflection. These consequences for the notion of regression are suggested by the empirical and systematic orders of psychoanalytic inquiry. Those who would still insist on placing this notion in the second order of definition, however, might review their approach in the light of classical metapsychology which puts regression, together with its conceptual twin of fixation as derived from libido theory,[11] at the fifth order of the present structure. But neither Freud nor any post-Freudians, from character analysts of the late twenties to ego psychologists of thirties and interpersonal therapists of the forties, ever used the notion of regression as an operational definition at the same order of significance as transference, resistance, anxiety, and they never tried to impose it on direct observation by any structure of inquiry. More or less gingerly, they all treated it as highly speculative and interpretive by way of fifth-order metapsychology. Although, in practice, a particular patient may follow the lead of his psychoanalyst's metapsychology or irregular terminology, and be observed to refer to himself as regressing, careful study of such observation usually reveals unintegrated anxiety along with transference and resistance, whose original sources may be historical but whose meaning relates to the ongoing failure of his efforts toward more congruous integration of the therapeutic field. In the present structure, therapeutic uses of regression are frequently definable as a particular patient's response to the very personal requirements of a particular psychoanalyst, and not as empirical or systematic constituents of his experience of therapy. In response to countertransference, moreover, the appearance of regression may become unavoidable in a particular psychoanalyst's work with a particular patient, and therefore may be expected to have complex and cumulative effects on the experiential field of therapy. The psychoanalyst who consciously decides to regress his patient, however, has to take a relativity view of the ensuing convergence of transference and countertransference, resistance and counterresistance, anxiety and counteranxiety, treat his patient's response as a response to regressive procedures and, if possible, even cooperate in fully exploring the therapeutic background of that psychological transaction.

Consider second-order definitions, now, in relation to third-order postulates. This is of methodological importance, coordinating first-order observations, as defined, with the explanatory theory at the fourth order. It is this relation of definitions to postulates, moreover, which makes empirical movement from the first to the second order so significant, for the rationale of this movement is to supply the systematic side of psychoanalytic structure wtih defined observations. Without moving from the first to the second order, indeed, discursive analysis of psychoanalytic experience itself would not be possible. Without it, there is simply nothing to talk about, let alone define, transform, explain or interpret. Although it is true that a total field of experience is other than the sum of its processes and patterns, since some are unanalyzable and others cannot be simultaneously analyzed, it is also true, nonetheless, that still others can be discursively analyzed. Otherwise, direct observations of transference and countertransference, for example, are literally as various and practically as myriad as all personal qualities of all psychoanalysts and all their patients. And finally, this transition from direct to defined observation orders and organizes the initially chaotic and eventually complex observation of gross experience. A psychoanalytic structure, without it, would be reduced to mere phenomenological description. It would take as long, at the very least, to review a psychoanalytic experience as it would to carry it through, and a tape recording would then have to be judged superior to any transformational analysis of processes and patterns—which, of course, turns therapy into anarchy.

Strictly from a structural point of view, an operational definition of empirical terms need not ordinarily be introduced, as such, into the actual experience of psychoanalytic therapy. Nothing new is usually added to the patient's understanding of his transfer of affective communication, for example, by his psychoanalyst simply calling it a defined observation of transference. The extremely anxious patient tends to receive it as a negative judgment which spells disapproval and rejection, the dominantly resistive patient tends to oppose or, by ignoring, to counter it in favor of his prior communication, and the well defended transferential patient tends to receive it as an invitation to engage in theoretical discourse. Within the ordered structure, then, operational definitions are shorthand references which direct a psychoanalyst's attention to other significant orders of inquiry, but when they also begin to direct a patient's attention away from affective and cognitive aspects of his original communication, they quickly lose their utility for empirical psychoanalytic inquiry. Obviously, it is just because of distortions, disturbances and difficulties that a patient cannot easily attend to significant processes and patterns of his psychology. Directly introduced as such into the therapeutic field, however, operational definitions tend to distract his probing curiosity from the pursuit of intensive inquiry, stimulate comments such as, "Oh! That's my transference!" or "There I go—resisting again!" and, depending on his problem, even turn the inquiry to superficial concerns. The patient does not undertake psychoanalysis to master the structure of its inquiry but, rather, the problems of his experience. And it remains to be established in fact that, for successful work with his patient's distortions, disturbances and difficulties, a psychoanalyst need achieve conscious mastery of this or any other structure of psychoanalytic inquiry—any more than a good artist, for example, need achieve conscious mastery of the physics of light and color. Substitutions of terminology for substance, it is clear, soon become hardened testimonials to a learned ignorance of psychoanalysis. Abuses of this sort hardly make a terminology superfluous, but it is still necessary for the practicing psychoanalyst to remain alert, however, to limitations and dangers which arise from free and easy reliance on the therapeutic power of sheer terminology.

To summarize: Second-order definitions of empirical terms are shorthand references to the operation of significant psychoanalytic processes and patterns. If, before inquiry in the particular case, it is known that resistance is generally a function of transference, then it is useful to consider the probable operation of one in the other's presence. If, furthermore, it is known before inquiry that a felt lack of integrative activity signals the emergence of anxiety, especially when it has not yet emerged as gross experience, then it is appropriate to postpone other therapeutic efforts. Or if it is known, finally, that psychoanalytic structure is realized in experiential fields of therapy, then even though the psychoanalyst may still be unclear about his countertransference, and even though his patient has not yet observed or described its impact on him, it is necessary to remain generally aware that any of the patient's communications may be treated as responses to the psychoanalyst's participation in the shared experience. In these three examples, a reliable judgment about transference, resistance, anxiety or counteranxiety, counterresistance, countertransference can become therapeutically significant during all phases of inquiry. While the direct use of second-order definitions does not alter experiences for which they are shorthand references, these definitions do provide the critical psychoanalyst with a sound empirical base, however, from which to elaborate the structure of his inquiry. They provide him with the necessary grist for third-order transformations which, together with fourth-order explanation, make it possible to intensify and systematize actual inquiry into the first order of direct observation—and, when he so inclines, even to affirm his own particular perspective on a patient's experience at the fifth order of interpretation. The logic of these second-order definitions may be called operational, therefore, in the strict sense that the psychoanalyst uses them to define direct observation of gross experience and coordinate these definitions with the third-order postulates by which he later transforms defined observations. That is, empirical activities of observation and definition prepare the ground for engaging, afterward, in systematic activities to make these defined observations intelligible in accordance with selected postulates, established theory and preferred metapsychology.

(3) *Transformation*

In the third order are general postulates. These provide for analysis of operational definitions, still more refined analysis of defined observations, and the most reliable means now available to organize results of these analyses into a body of knowledge. Since postulates govern the study of recurrent relations among second-order definitions, they therefore most closely approximate the instrumental and systematic methods of laboratory experimentation. In structured inquiry, the point of obtaining first-order observations whose operation may be defined as transference, resistance, anxiety and counteranxiety, counterresistance, countertransference is not to exercise the application of second-order terms. The point is, of course, to infer by postulate transformations the existence of unobserved processes and patterns from the functional relations which these have to processes and patterns already observed in previous inquiry. The significance of postulate transformations for the overall structure of psychoanalysis resides in their power to coordinate observations which are made of transference, for example, with those to be made of resistance, both transference and resistance with those to be made of anxiety, counteranxiety with those to be made of counterresistance, or both counteranxiety and counterresistance with those to be made of countertransference. Their significance also resides in their power to coordinate observations of transference, resistance, anxiety with those of counteranxiety, counterresistance, countertransference, so that the defined operation of one guides further inquiry to observation of selected others. While this does not always check out in each individual case, no postulate is set aside by such failed predictions until, in accordance with empirical and systematic requirements, a more fruitful one is formulated which applies to an equal or greater number of cases.

Although postulates govern the transformation of defined observations, they are themselves neither direct observations, however, nor operational definitions. Instead, they are posited in order to explore and coordinate observations and definitions, and their systematic utility rests on the agreement which then obtains between expected relations among defined observations and actual results of further inquiry. If anxiety is observed and defined, for example, and if through one or more postulates the operation of transference is then inferred, systematic utility

of the postulates is tested by later determinations that transference is or is not observable. In the psychoanalytic structure,
therefore, general postulates are assigned to the third order of
inquiry and are clearly differentiated from second-order definitions in that no empirical operation with first-order observations performs their connective service; they alone supply the
required systematic operations. The notion that second-order
definitions are coordinated, moreover, cannot itself be represented or confirmed by any direct observations of gross experience. In structuring his inquiry, the psychoanalyst introduces this notion to guide the use of general postulates. The
task he assumes of making observations differs, in this radical
sense, from that of providing a warrant for the relations he can
demonstrate to exist among them. It is not simply that he is
capable of observing of transference and resistance, however,
after observing anxiety. It is, rather, that he actively seeks to
observe transference and resistance after observing anxiety.
To guide transformations necessary for this, he uses third-order
postulates of genesis and function, structure and dynamism,
immediacy and reflection—as well, of course, as the fourth-order
theory of unconscious experience—in order to observe and define why the patient is anxious and cannot ordinarily sustain
relatedness and communication, and in order to transform,
explain and perhaps interpret it as a particular phase of the
psychoanalytic experience.

But general postulates are not empirically given. They do not
take the form of asserting the existence of anything in particular but, rather, that of intervening principles to coordinate
second-order definitions into conditional propositions and transform their range of application to first-order observations.
These postulates, moreover, do not support statements about the
nature of the human psyche or, as such, provide descriptions of
directly observable processes and patterns. Instead, they expe-

dite the psychoanalysis of gross experience by effecting reliable
relations among defined observations and by guiding reliable
transformations of them. To delineate the third order of
postulation, therefore, is to control psychoanalytic inquiry by
drawing the line between its systematic and empirical concerns.
The postulate of genesis, for example, is not the same as the
historical sense which every patient usually has about familial
and childhood origins of his problems. By this postulate, the
psychoanalyst does not develop inquiry into history to enforce
his patient's common sense notion about the origins of his
psychological problems but, he expects, to obtain historical
information about a second-order definition. Then, he either
coordinates that definition with another or applies still other
postulates for further transformations of the history—and, at
later stages, may also apply the fourth-order theory. To adopt
the patient's commonsense notion of origins when, for example,
he is undergoing a turbulent experience of anxiety, actually
abuses the postulate of genesis, because defined observations of
anxiety ordinarily are better explored under the postulate of
immediacy, as the felt lack of integrative activity in shared experience which reflects a set of unidentified conditions in the
unconscious present. If, to explore anxiety, genetic analysis is
not reserved until these unconscious conditions in the present
are awarely articulated, then appeal to history loses its felt
immediacy. It does not facilitate therapeutic movement to a
more open study of experienced anxiety or its genuine and distorted components in current fields of inquiry. This is not to
say that, in response to anxiety, appeal to history is not indi-
cated in all structures of psychotherapeutic inquiry, since some
short-term, nondirective, hypnotic and other psychotherapies
do not make anxiety a major definition of their structures.
But this is to say, rather, that turning away from the patient's
current anxieties in relation to his psychoanalyst does not

realize the psychoanalytic structure or result in psychoanalytic experience.

During actual clinical inquiry, general postulates differ from metapsychology in that they are directly governed by sequences of psychological processes and patterns which can be both observed and defined by psychological means. These postulates do not merely render faithful phenomenological readings of past, present or expected experience; they also support and expand the use of operational definitions of certain observable aspects of processes and patterns. For when some of these aspects are directly observed, it is possible to infer the existence of others which are not directly observed, well defined or based on previous information. General postulates, then, are the principles of transformation. From an external point of view, they may be criticized as being too abstract, simple or vague, yet they remain the best structural tools now available for constructing and organizing psychoanalytic inquiry around its fourth-order theory of unconscious experience. Their future, however, is by no means fixed in accordance with their past utility. New information from other psychologies and other sciences, first of all, may suggest ways to improve the structure of psychoanalytic inquiry, but since the direct study of live experience has features which are peculiar to itself, this is not a likely prospect in the near future. Second, the ongoing search for new defined observations which have the firm reliability of transference, resistance, anxiety and counteranxiety, counterresistance, countertransference, if successful, may require such basic changes in the set of general postulates as to change the overall structure of inquiry. And third, the probability is that discovery of new relationships among these well established terms will root them more firmly in the experiential field of psychoanalytic therapy.

In different contexts, some postulates are more significantly applied than others. One may provide a more inclusive field of observation as, for example, the postulate of structure which can relate defined observations of transference and counter-transference in order to explore more thoroughly a patient's involvements with his psychoanalyst and a psychoanalyst's involvements with his patient. Another may produce a transformation of therapeutic inquiry which makes it possible to attempt more precise and focused observations than any individual operational definitions as, for example, the postulate of genesis relating defined observations of transference and resistance to provide a historical basis for studying those oppositional movements of awareness which, in some distorted and disturbed sense, seem to cope with difficulties encountered in therapeutic experience. Postulate transformations prove effective, then, if they so relate second-order definitions that further inquiry supports inferences about previously defined observations and if, of course, they also support the reliable application of fourth-order theory. Their usage remains contingent on the overall psychoanalytic structure, however, only in so far as this structure becomes evident in clinical inquiry, and not as a matter of preference or preconception. Third-order postulates fall into pairs, genesis and function, structure and dynamism, immediacy and reflection, and they are stated in this sequence. The postulate of genesis is:

G   Historical and developmental aspects of psychological
           processes and patterns are subsumed under the postulate
           of genesis. They provide the basis for understanding both
           the rise of processes and the development of current pat-
           terns in various fields of experience and through various
           stages of growth.

Note, here, that the use of genetic analysis requires theoretical assumptions about the organization of personality which, it is clear, involve metapsychologies at the fifth order. Because existing metapsychologies tend to vary so widely, however, there is no point to making a more concrete statement of this postulate. Aside from the functional autonomies, moreover, there are difficulties experienced and manifested in transference, resistance, anxiety which need not be studied exclusively in the light of past developmental conditioning—which cannot even be studied in this way as long as, in principle, useful information about current difficulties may also be obtained from the expected and still unrealized future. Historical postdictions have been proposed, it is true, as influencing the direction of psychological change. But from this influence, it is not possible to derive the systematic basis of its therapeutic effects on the direction of change. Although empirically observed, it is possible to derive this influence, simply, from the abiding faith of unconscious social experience that understanding the past has special and crucial explanatory power. But the psychoanalytic structure, in any case, requires this postulate of genesis, even when the particular psychoanalyst leaves questions of metapsychology to his patients, because it governs the study of natural dimensions of observation which are defined in therapeutic inquiry. The postulate of function is:

F   The action and reaction of processes and patterns, as these produce a nexus with others within the experiential field in which they appear, are studied by the postulate of function. It characterizes both the relatedness and the communication of processes and patterns.

There is, of course, a large biological substrate to the human capacity to undergo psychoanalysis, but its study rightfully belongs to biology. This capacity does not directly depend, moreover, on the possession of a special brain, the ability to use the constituents of language, or the development of emotional intelligence. It depends, simply and generically, on human functioning. Aside, however, from the biological or the physical, there are significant functional aspects of process and pattern which, as psychological, can be studied under the conditions of psychoanalytic inquiry. No functional aspect in statement F possesses psychoanalytic meaning, of course, apart from the genetic aspects in statement G while, in conjunction with the structural aspects in statement S, it relates varieties of process and pattern to the integrative basis of their function. The postulate of structure is:

S   Structure is described in terms of its constituent processes and patterns, integrative contexts of inquiry, fields of experience or human situations. This postulate denotes the meaningfully organized aspects of connected and mutually dependent psychological processes and patterns.

The meaning of a structure is not always, of course, a simple sum of the meanings of its constituent processes and patterns. A study of discrete processes and patterns which make up defined observations of transference, resistance, anxiety and counteranxiety, counterresistance, countertransference without a structural assessment of their constituents in relation to both the organized personality and the experiential field of therapy, cannot have significant psychoanalytic results. For the qualities of a whole structure, moreover, are never identical with those of its individual constitutents. The structural aspects of psychological process and pattern as a whole are distinct—no less, clearly, than its genetic and functional aspects—from those of its analyzed constituents. Note, here, that process is considered a constituent of pattern, pattern a constituent of structure, structure a constituent of personality. As a matter of ordered inquiry, structure is neither made nor invented but encountered and described. Its study at the third order, therefore, puts psychoanalytic inquiry on the solid base of ongoing experience, avoiding the extreme of irrational romanticism in which observation and definition are merely the free acts of anarchic will and the extreme of existentialist mysticisms which turn these first two orders of inquiry into transcendental oddities. A transformation of structure, then, is made in terms of the character a process or pattern is observed to possess, constituents it is defined to exhibit, and activities it sustains in actual clinical inquiry. The postulate of dynamism is:

D   Dynamism embraces any psychological reason why particular processes or patterns modify the direction of experience toward satisfaction of needs, realization of goals and fulfillment of ideals. It studies that psychological striving which subtends the means-ends continuum.

The problem of instincts, drives and energy transformations is not methodologically relevant to the empirical or systematic inquiry of psychoanalysis. This problem belongs at the fifth order of metapsychology, and it belongs there because no psychological means known to date can determine the relation of instincts, drives or energy transformations to the live communication and direction of experience in therapy. Thus far, established psychological inquiry is capable at best of providing only tentative determinations of feelings, thoughts and attitudes in relation to contexts of personal, interpersonal and social experience. By this postulate, therefore, it is asserted that wish, impulse or striving subtends the productive unfolding of human capacities and guides attention, intelligence and behavior to the enstatement of workable means and the consummation of desirable ends—within the perspective of satisfying personal and organic needs, realizing interpersonal and social goals, and fulfilling humanist and universal ideals. The postulate of immediacy is:

I   Directly presented affect, unrehearsed and noncognitive impulse and both qualitative and unanalyzable aspects of psychological contexts of process and pattern are treated by the postulate of immediacy. Immediate affect and impulse provide the integrating thread during inquiry for closure, synthesis and consummatory experience.

There is a hard difference between analyzable and unanalyzable aspects of mind, self and experience which are observed to occur in the immediate mode, and a large and almost invariable therapeutic issue is to determine this difference in empirical terms. The immediate aspects are communicated in expressive as distinct from referential and reflective symbols, even though communication studied under this postulate may be transformed and later defined as derivatives of processes and patterns which previously were outside the scope of awareness. This postulate of immediacy resembles the other five, however, in that it also acquires its full sense and appropriateness in conjunction with them. By the postulate of function, for example, symbols of immediate experience may be found to have been only functionally immediate and, by the postulate of structure, to have possessed referential and reflective constituents. At first expressed and described as direct experiences of transference, resistance, anxiety or counteranxiety, counter-resistance, countertransference, when their unconscious dimensions are explored, they may be revealed to have possessed the referential and reflective constituents in past formations of their patterns. They may be found, that is, to be made up of referential and reflective as well as expressive symbols. But even after these and other postulate transformations, there remain symbols of immediate experience which do not yield to modification. In any phase of the inquiry, some immediate qualities of experience continue to be directly observed as expressing individual differences in temperament and body rhythm, and they remain observable throughout every phase to the close of the entire inquiry. In this respect, the postulate of immediacy has a crucial point in psychoanalytic structure.

For without it or one like it, psychoanalysis becomes literally interminable and even infinite—ever searching for ever unattainable finis or terminus, synthesis or resolution—because the analytic mode would have no place to rest. The postulate of reflection is:

R   Indirect and representational thought, rehearsed and cognitive inference and both mediating and analyzable aspects of psychological processes and patterns are treated by the postulate of reflection. It focuses on logical and rational aspects of the experience of therapy.

If personal knowledge arising from the defined observations of the first two orders is to survive and integrate as new experience, its organization requires the use of logic and reason, and reflective intelligence is the creative guide to this end. Unlike expressive symbols of immediacy or referential symbols of observation, reflective symbols are far more complex cognitive phenomena, involving logical and rational relations of symbols to one another. That is, a patient's use of expressive symbols may stretch all the way from "Ah!" on relaxing during a session, to the chatter of teeth during an unexpected encounter with anxiety; his referential use of symbols describes one or another aspect of his relations to himself or to his environment, as in, "That is an anxious man!" or "He becomes sadistic and destructive about the expression of feeling"; and his reflective use of symbols denotes cognitive relations among symbols involving elements of logical and rational thought, as in, "To know oneself is to be free to experience" or "Reconstruction of the distorted self depends on analysis of transference." In addition, therefore, to relating some symbols to direct expression and others to objective reference, the postulate of reflection provides for relations among these uses of symbols during phases of inquiry which are undertaken to establish logical and rational contexts of feeling, attitude and thought in various fields of inquiry. This postulate invokes well established methods of reasoning—like those, for example, of agreement and difference, probability and empirical generalization—in order to integrate varieties of experience, their meanings in particular fields of therapy and their implicit probabilities for the direction of psychological change.

So much for the proposed postulates of psychoanalytic inquiry: Consider, now, some overall features of their outline as the third order. First, it reconstructs a major classical point of view—topography; second, it restates others—genesis, structure, dynamism; third, it includes new postulates—function, immediacy, reflection; and fourth, it excludes still others—the economic point of view of the early biological perspective and the adaptive point of view of the later modified biological perspective. Each of these overall features has its own rationale. First, the reconstruction: The topographical point of view originally described both areas and qualities of human experience, but after the systematic unconscious was taken from this point of view and made the id of the classical structural point of view, topography was still used to ascribe unconscious qualities of psychological processes and patterns. The distinction of conscious from unconscious experience, however, may now be considered most significant for all psychoanalysis—far more, indeed, than any second-order definition or third-order postulate —and this point of view is therefore reconstructed as theory of unconscious experience and, as such, is separately treated at the fourth order of inquiry.

Second, the restatement: Because metapsychology is pluralistic at the fifth order of inquiry, it is both possible and necessary to reformulate the third order so that the meaning and application of its postulates are compatible with many perspectives on metapsychology which are adopted in psychoanalysis as philosophies of experience and value. One way of doing this, at present, is to restrict statements of the third order to psycho-

logical terms and conditions of inquiry, leaving their philosophy and value to the special perspective which a particular
psychoanalyst adopts at the fifth order and leaving room for
changes in their philosophy and value which derive from each
particular patient's response to it. Structure of inquiry is not
and, after all, should not be a philosophy of life. Its clear demarcation ought to be accomplished, therefore, so that it is not
directly dependent on the therapeutic metapsychology of any
individual or group practicing psychoanalysis. Although structure of inquiry goes hand in hand with interpretive metapsychology in actual psychoanalytic experience, a theory of this
therapy should indicate where the hard factuality of the former
is distinguished from the poetic metaphors of the latter. Psychology and values are experienced as being very closely related
in intrapersonal, interpersonal and transpersonal terms, but in
no sense does this indicate a basis for fusing or confusing the
two disciplines in the structure of psychoanalysis. Whatever
else may be said about psychology and values, it must be said
that they are distinct fields of inquiry. It is proposed, therefore, that analysis of empirical and systematic orders proceed
without introducing the interpretive and speculative order
until certain metatheories of psychology or metapsychologies
are openly brought into play.

Third, the inclusion: Postulates of function, immediacy and
reflection are being formulated at this order because of the
range of psychological observation they encompass as relevant
to psychoanalytic inquiry. The need for these postulates could
not become apparent when, in the model of id therapy, a
patient's experience of his psychoanalyst was predominantly
conceived as an after-image of his oedipal phase, and the organization of his personality was essentially based on the unfolding
of chaotic and timeless processes of his id. Considering, also,
that classical points of view were originally formulated in line

with such conceptions, it is difficult to understand why, in the thirties, new points of view or postulates were not also developed for the model of ego or interpersonal therapy to accommodate new ego and interpersonal facts which then became available to both the modified biological and the cultural wings of psychoanalysis. Instead, certain metapsychological perspectives such as the adaptive or adaptational points of view were introduced as postulates when, in fact, they were interpretive and speculative and, therefore, did not belong to this third order. They are fifth-order metapsychology, it is proposed, because they deal with philosophy of organism and environment, individual and culture, and so on—which certainly are interesting, significant and imaginative in their own right, even though they are not strictly psychological in empirical origin or systematic application.

If, on the other hand, the ego is no longer conceived as emerging from the id, or if developmental periods of the self other than infancy and childhood are now also relevant for therapeutic inquiry—that period, even, in which the patient enters and undergoes psychoanalysis—then some such postulate as that of function becomes necessary at the third order. It can expand the exploration of operational definitions, to apply them to these newer domains of psychoanalytic inquiry and therapy. Postulation of function is at least as important as that of genesis—whose value was fully realized, indeed, by the hypnocathartic therapists of the last century—since in a post-ego and post-interpersonal model of shared experience, a patient's problems may be as fruitfully explored in the light of his expected and still unlived future as in the light of his already realized but repressed past. No a priori judgment, it is clear, can possibly indicate which temporal dimension provides greater illumination in the particular case. But most important of all, the functional postulate covers those aspects of second-order definitions which cannot be solely studied in the focus of history. The postulate of reflection is required, obviously, by the many new discoveries of ego and interpersonal psychology which were made in the biological and cultural wings of psychoanalysis: It accounts for cognitive, logical and rational functions of the personal ego or interpersonal self. The postulate of immediacy, on the other hand, is required by more recent psychoanalytic inquiry as the study of personal psychology in direct action in the experiential field of therapy: It accounts for the directly had sense of self in the individualities of both participants, from which is derived an irreducible baseline for observation of self-actions, interactions and transactions, and by which personal differences of temperament and body rhythm are both felt in personal experience and made felt in the experience of others throughout every phase of psychoanalytic therapy. In the model of shared experience, this postulate serves to integrate directly felt aspects of transference, for example, with the structural impact of past processes and patterns being explored in current fields of inquiry. It makes both feasible and fruitful the observation of transference, resistance, anxiety and counteranxiety, counterresistance, countertransference along a temporal continuum stretching backward and forward, yet does not antecedently affirm the therapeutic utility of any one phase of this continuum as being superior to that of any other.

And fourth, the exclusion: The economic point of view is being partly replaced by the postulate of reflection and partly lifted to the fifth order of metapsychology. To the extent that a patient is capable of describing the increase or decrease or, more generally, the amount of one feeling in comparison with another, and to the extent that he is capable of attributing more or less anxiety to some processes and patterns than others, the postulate of reflection suffices to account for these quasi-quantitative differences. Although the existence of measurable quantities of psychic energy has long been defended in psychoanalytic theory, instruments do not yet exist for making useful measurements of psychological processes and patterns in the experiential field of therapy. From the fact that these instruments are not yet constructed, of course, it does not follow in logic or practice that they will never be constructed and successfully adapted. But even if they did exist, on the other hand, their successful adaptation to the experiential field of therapy need have no logical or practical effects on the psychoanalytic structure. Their results may still, of course, be subsumed under the postulate of reflection without, therefore, significantly altering the outcome as psychoanalytic experience. In the ongoing therapeutic inquiries of psychoanalysis, meanwhile, the use of reflective intelligence suffices for descriptions of both the quality and the intensity of quasi-quantitative differences which are open to correction as new observations are discursively made to discriminate among these different experiences.

Some perspectives on classical metapsychology explicitly require this economic point of view in order to work out relations among other points of view which support the notion that psychic energy has measurable units of reduction or transformation. But since metapsychology is neither empirical nor systematic but interpretive, this economic point of view may be posited at the fifth order with the proviso, only, that it is not directly applicable to empirical and systematic orders of the structure. Methodological difficulties arising from the direct use of rigorous mathematico-experimental methods in the ongoing psychoanalytic experience are huge, of course, and well known, and they seriously suggest that the economic point of view need no longer be numbered among the postulate transformations at the third order. It is not simply that the transactions of psychoanalytic inquiry in vivo cannot be measured—this fact alone would not, in principle, prove to be an insuperable obstacle to the postulation of their measurable character—but, rather, that useful quantification would require such narrowing of the units of observation to conscious processes and patterns under strictly controlled conditions as to narrow the usefulness of its results. Clinically, however, the problem of every psychoanalytic experience is far more complex. When, for example, the patient undergoes particularly disorienting experiences of anxiety—even if, per impossible, all other conditions in and around the therapeutic field could be held constant—a quantitative analysis would not begin to reveal the structure or function of that anxiety in the organization of his personality. Nor would it, in fact, begin to touch its immediate and reflective significance in current fields of his shared experience. The classical distinction of primary from secondary processes is far more useful, indeed, for dealing with this complexity in clinical inquiry.

When, as a further example, the patient expresses affective attitudes about his psychoanalyst, whatever else he may be conceived as doing, he is actually expressing attitudes with direct and immediate impact. But since these attitudes are communicable, they also are in some sense analyzable during appropriate phases of the inquiry. At the third order of psychoanalytic structure, their constituents may be analyzed in accordance with the six postulates of genesis and function, structure and dynamism, immediacy and reflection. Even as organized, however, experience of their primary processes remains immediate, affective and noncognitive and, as such, is unanalyzable. In this sense, as primary, the most that can be determined about these processes are conditions and transformations in and through which they occur and, because of this, they are well termed prototaxic. They are present with similar force in, for example, both the infants gurgling and the adult's sense of glee, regardless of the very dissimilar conditions in which these prototaxic constituents can be observed to occur. As organized experience, moreover, the secondary patterns of these affective attitudes are reflective and cognitive, among other things, and therefore become readily analyzable. Patterned, they may distortedly occur in the reflective foreground of therapeutic inquiry and, yet, also arise from functional conditions of genetic development and structural organization. Such transformations of primary processes and secondary patterns, then, may all be distributed under postulates of the third order. In actual psychoanalytic inquiry, of course, processes and patterns which are later distinguished as primary and secondary do not just emerge so labelled in a pure state, from which it is clear that their classical distinction was not originally made as empirical observation. If wider postulations can cover the same clinical phenomena and others as well, moreover, the distinction itself may now be considered necessary only for the classical model of id therapy. This tack is justified, furthermore, by the fact that it makes for a clearer, simpler yet more inclusive structure of psychoanalytic inquiry.

Recall, at this point, an earlier comment about the adaptive point of view. No postulate of adaptation need be formulated at the third order, it was suggested, because it would involve assumptions about organism and environment or individual and culture which are strictly the concerns of fifth-order metapsychology whose scope extends from biology and biological metaphor to explicit analyses of social organization, cultural values and philosophic ideals. For the same reason, the treatment of such notions as instinct theory, drive reduction and energy transformation is restricted to the fifth order. Nor, for that matter, are any third-order postulates of psychic determinism or its alternatives of conditioning and spontaneity being formulated either, because these are all properly the concerns of interpretive and speculative metapsychology whose scope may even extend to a statement of what "it" is that makes the structure of psychoanalytic inquiry possible, or of what "it" is that makes useful results of psychoanalytic therapy probable. Both the implications and the alternatives of psychic determinism belong to the order of metapsychology in the same way that, in other sciences, physical determinism and its implications and alternatives belong to the order of metaphysics. They are not being so treated as third-order postulation, of course, because of their interpretive and speculative character as metatheory. In so far as they do not produce genuine confusion of the third order, however, their utility still remains an open question. To this order in the structure, psychoanalytic inquiry does not require them while later, at the fifth order, philosophic judgment decides the controversial questions about their necessity. The relevance of psychic determinism to empirical and systematic inquiry, thus far, is not a matter of fact but belief. It differs, furthermore, from the relevance of such notions as cause and effect which may be studied under the defined terms of observation and which, consequently, are interchangeable with these defined terms. Psychic determinism is essentially metapsychology, then, whose empirical and systematic status in the experiential field of psychoanalytic inquiry is itself indeterminate. Wherefore, any two psychoanalysts may hold even opposing views of it or its alternatives and still cooperate in organizing and developing the first four orders of structured inquiry. Only at the fifth order do metapsychologists have to deal with it one way or another in psychoanalysis.

Note, also, that distortion is not being treated as operational definition of the second order or postulate of the third order. Surprising, perhaps, but certainly illuminating, this development is a direct result of viewing psychoanalysis as structure of inquiry. The notion of distortion need not be ordered as definition or postulate because distorted qualities of any defined observation may be derived from more intensive study which relates that observation to third-order postulates and fourth-order theory. This accomplishes two valuable objectives. First, of course, it makes for both simplicity and clarity in the structure of inquiry. And second, the psychoanalyst does not have to decide, in advance of his patient's communication or his own fifth order, what ails his patient and how it is to be interpreted. Instead, they can work together toward not only the resolution of distortion but its definition as well. In the case of transference, for example, the distinction of its qualities as genuine and distorted may be systematically derived by studying genesis, first, to check its historical roots in various stages of development; second, function to check its relations to its other manifestations as well as to those of resistance, anxiety, counteranxiety and so on; third, structure to check relations among its constituent processes and to other patterns of process in the organization of personality; fourth, dynamism to check its relations to forward striving and movement for satisfaction of needs, realization of goals and fulfillment of ideals; fifth, immediacy to check its irreducible as distinct from its modifiable processes and patterns; and sixth, reflection to check its logical and symbolic relations to other such processes and patterns. Yet, most significant for the psychoanalytic as distinct from other psychotherapeutic structures is the application of fourth-order theory of unconscious experience to the results of these postulate transformations in order, now, to specify defined observations of transference which are beyond the scope of awareness—in turn, forgotten history and repressed development by the postulate of genesis; parataxic communication and disjunctive relatedness by that of function; underdeveloped pattern and unintegrated organization by that of structure; frustrated needs, failed goals and unfulfilled ideals by that of dynamism; distorted feeling and incongrouous impulse by that of immediacy; irrational observation and illogical inference by that of reflection.[12] As observed to occur in psychoanalytic fields of therapy, of course, the relations of transference to resistance, anxiety and counteranxiety, counterresistance, counter-transference may also be checked, singly or jointly, partly or wholly, by application of these six postulates and this theory. Clearly, analysis of transference is a very varied, complex and cumulative procedure, and is not ordinarily terminated before the closing phases of therapeutic experience. A judgment of its genuine and distorted qualities, it is also clear, does not require other second-order definitions or third-order postulates than those which have already been presented. Yet, this judgment cannot be made to stick without, however, also introducing the distinction of conscious from unconscious experience which is formulated as the fourth-order theory and suffices for the empirical field of psychoanalytic inquiry.

Full postulate transformation, as outlined here, is rarely accomplished in the particular case. It is a matter of personal psychology and perspective on metapsychology that the particular psychoanalyst tends to select certain postulates more frequently than others—to the extent, at least, that his procedure is consciously pursued—in the intensive study of distortions in perception, disturbances in awareness and difficulties in living. What is required of him during any particular phase of therapeutic inquiry, however, is not deducible from this or any other proposed psychoanalytic structure. In the study of any particular patient's experience, this is so because it is not possible to enstate clearly controlled conditions under which to make reliable predictions in practice. The transfer of experience is sometimes dramatic and recurrent, usually fragmentary and piecemeal, often shadowy and indistinct, and no known method is capable of predicting its exact occurrence in time and place or quality and content since, as a complex patterning of processes, its specific manifestations are subject to myriad variables—most of which are, in fact, beyond the psychoanalyst's experimental control and the patient's self-aware direction. This outlined structure of postulate transformation may be viewed, therefore, as representing limits of psychological inquiry under which it is now possible to invoke the psychoanalytic theory of unconscious experience. And since distinction of the distorted from the genuine can thus be systematically derived, instead of being simply defined at the second order or postulated at the third, the standard of simplicity in systematic formulation would favor this shaving down of excess terminology and analysis. Even after defined observations are worked through the third and fourth orders and then transformed and explained as more genuine than distorted, or the other way around, the systematic results still fail to suggest any reasons why these processes and patterns are the way they are in human experience. These results do not answer the question of why, in theory, they generally behave the ways they do during psychoanalytic therapy or why, in fact, they are susceptible of observation and definition, transformation and explanation. There still is no satisfactory psychological reason, by the same token, which explains why change takes place, and so psychological change is neither defined at the second order nor postulated at the third. The reasons which are ordinarily given for it in psychoanalysis are, of course, essentially metapsychological. But third-order postulates do concern observations and definitions of processes and patterns, however, in which change takes place. Those of genesis and function, for example, provide a basis for deriving statements about the changing conditions of time and place, while those of dynamism and reflection provide a basis for deriving statements about aims and directions of such change. Postulate transformations at best, however, only imply or intimate interpretations, the point of these transformations being to structure a possible application of the psychoanalytic theory of unconscious experience and to assign their interpretation to philosophy and values, about which ideal speculation is more valid than natural observation. Metapsychologies of the past usually become efforts, at some point, to develop reasons why backward and forward movement always takes place and, as part of these efforts, to decide among competing claims to the interpretation of psychological change. Some examples of these interpretations are: sexual theory of personality development, archetypes of the collective unconscious, power theory of inferiority and protest, assertions of the pure will, and so on. Human experience may also be regarded, however, as having all these as well as other generic traits because, in fact, it is no more than experience and no less than human. This view does not supply any exclusive reasons why human experience is what it is, or any necessary bond for these to the exclusion of any other speculative visions in the structure of psychoanalytic inquiry. And in order to leave at least some interpretation of the patient's experience to the patient himself, the relation of psychology and values in psychoanalytic therapy is briefly summarized: The psychoanalyst centers his work in therapy on the empirical and systematic structure of his inquiry and, in affirmation of certain scientific and humanist values, makes room for his patient to make his own interpretations of life.

Reconsider, finally, that selection of these six postulates for a structure of inquiry does not put them in tacit tandem or necessary connection to any single metapsychology. Before the fifth order, this structure does not explictly include philosophies of experience or theories of value, and it does not exlicitly depend on selected postulates and corollaries which learning and experimental psychologies apply in their structures of inquiry. A psychoanalytic fact which is derived by empirical and systematic inquiry is, no doubt, a species of psychological fact—no more, no less than the results of animal and human experiment of these other psychologies are other species of psychological fact. But it is not possible to remove psychoanalytic facts from their context of structured inquiry and, without careful modification, transfer their interpretive usage to other structures of psychological inquiry. Nor is it possible, by the same token, to apply facts gained by psychological experiment directly to psychoanalysis as structure of inquiry or experience of therapy without, also, submitting these facts to careful modification. For the special purposes of special circumstances, practicing psychoanalysts may invoke the experimental results of any science, of course, as well as fictional characterizations of literature and commonsense views of the humanities, in order to influence the patient in directions which they judge constructive. Only as they work within the boundaries of their ordered structure of inquiry, clearly, are they on the firm grounds of empirical and systematic psychoanalysis. Even when they work toward the realization of this structure, however, they may have to rely on these sorts of intervention in certain fields of therapy. Yet, they may also find it useful to distinguish the reliable knowledge they offer, as psychoanalysts, from dramatized states of emotion which they often stimulate by these various speculative means of interpretation. It may be argued, of course, that any proposed structure of psychoanalytic inquiry is embedded in one or another interpretive metapsychology, whether or not the relationship is openly articulated. And about this, obviously, there need be no disagreement. But there is a clear difference between any proposed structure of psychoanalytic inquiry being embedded in one or another interpretive metapsychology, no matter how that is, and orders of inquiry being demarcated within the structure such that their statements are not all metapsychological in form or content. As proposed, then, statements of the postulates are set forth with this end in view—to put the psychoanalytic structure in order.

It is to be hoped, of course, that all postulates and theories of all psychologies will one day be coordinated into an over-arching framework. This may even include, perhaps, fictional characterizations of literature and commonsense views of the humanities, as well as postulates and theories of impinging social and biological sciences and, finally, speculations and beliefs of philosophy and theology. But that day is by no means near at hand—even if, reasonably, it were assumed that the task is reasonable. Within the field of psychology alone, for example, common elements of various approaches and results are not yet sufficiently clear and, therefore, are not yet essentially agreed upon for clear formulation. Some psychoanalytic meta-psychologies have attempted answers to this problem, but until they filter through various structures of psychological inquiry and, perhaps, into unconscious cultural attitudes about the nature of the human psyche as well, it is doubtful that they actually provide the illumination claimed for them. Although well articulated, these metapsychologies do not exhaust all possible or probable visions of human experience, moreover, which are compatible with the structure of psychoanalytic inquiry. To establish the utility of any, finally, it is necessary and appropriate to begin by first putting psychoanalysis in order. For if this first effort does not succeed, why expect any psychoanalytic metapsychology to put all psychology in order—or, even, the whole culture—and do it in a universal way?

(4) *Explanation*

At the fourth order is the integrative theory of psychoanalytic inquiry. Formulated, here, is the most general systematic principle of psychoanalysis which integrates postulate transformations and defined observations for the purpose of relating new psychological conditions to the study of problematic experience which the patient originally presents. It holds, in theory, that every experiental field of therapy contains some unconscious processes and patterns, and it is:

U   Psychoanalytic inquiry enlarges the scope of awareness of psychological information which clarifies problems in living. This information spans the repressed, distorted and unrealized processes and patterns of past, present and future experience, and is used to reintegrate those in with those outside awareness.

This theory points up the logical purpose of organizing a structure of psychoanalytic inquiry and, in practice, differentiates this inquiry from the other psychotherapeutic inquiries. In psychology and philosophy, there are many approaches to the study of human experience which also take account of unconscious experience both in and around the clinical field of inquiry. Since the turn of the century, however, when psychoanalysis first emerged as organized inquiry, this theory has received increasing acceptance and confirmation in most psychologies and philosophies But no other field, regardless of its ultimate interpretation of unconscious experience, ever attempts to be as thorough or far-reaching as psychoanalysis in applying this theory to distortions in perception, disturbances in awareness and difficulties in living.

The psychoanalytic field of inquiry, from its early beginnings, may be defined by a quest for structured inquiry in which distinctions of conscious from unconscious experience dominate the therapeutic study of psychological problems. Originally rooted in the hypnoid states of hypnocathartic therapy, this theory of unconscious experience has since evolved in accordance with three models of therapy—id, ego or interpersonal, shared experience. In response to these changing models, various orders of psychoanalytic structure have all undergone many changes of form, content and relationship for the sake of sharpening their statement and expanding their application. The fourth order of theory, however, remains a central guideline to the formulation of third-order postulates which transform observations made at the first order and defined at the second. By this theory, it is first asserted that human experience cannot be wholly explained by the processes and patterns of interpersonal and social behavior which are available to conscious awareness and, second, that the resolution of personal problems can never be exclusively accomplished in terms of interpersonal and social awareness and behavior. Accordingly, a theory of unconscious experience is set forth in psychoanalysis which explains the processes and patterns of distortion, disturbance and difficulty within awareness by the discovery of others beyond awareness and, therefore, beyond ordinary observation and definition prior to therapeutic inquiry. On the basis of this theory, it is possible to seek the meaning of unconsciously transferred processes and patterns, for example, in unconscious processes and patterns of resistance or anxiety. It is also possible, furthermore, to derive the unconscious relativity of transference and countertransference by the application of this theory to the defined observations of either or both, which are then amenable to postulate transformations.

To transform unconscious into conscious experience is clearly then, by established theory, the main focus of psychoanalytic inquiry and therapy. This is why the relations of defined observations both to one another and to general postulates have always been organized for the maximal application of fourth-order theory in the experiential field of therapy. In other words, statements from the first to the fourth orders constitute a structure of knowledge which, in itself, suffices for all empirical and systematic applications of this psychological theory—in so far, of course, as these applications derive from the structure. The description of gross experience which can be observed in actual psychoanalytic therapy ordinarily suffices for establishing the operation of second-order definitions, while their coordination with third-order postulates suffices, as well, for establishing transformations of these defined observations. But the explanatory power of the overall structure of clinical psychoanalytic inquiry, however, is located and justified at this fourth order of theory. Although this power is now limited, it will most probably expand with the eventual increase of second-order definitions and, then, with appropriate modifications and additions of third-order postulates. In present knowledge, meanwhile, reliability of psychoanalytic assertions about problems in living should be confined to the warrant of psychoanalytic structure as it is now constituted around this fourth-order theory of unconscious experience.

In the serial order of psychoanalysis, the point is to establish determinate meanings of this fourth-order theory for problems of gross experience which are selected by direct observation, specified by operational definition and transformed by postulate analysis. While certain types of observed, defined and transformed experience provide factual evidence for applying this theory, other types of gross experience are still beyond its compass. If certain experience—described, now, as absurdity, emptiness or confusion—ever is properly observed, defined and transformed, it may eventually require modifications of the theory. But in view of the observations already defined, transformed and explained and the relative solidity of the whole structure, it is doubtful that psychoanalysis of unconscious psychology as a field of inquiry will ever be entirely displaced. It may have different names, acquire new definitions, postulates and metapsychologies, modify its structure beyond virtual recognition or, even, recede into wider theories which encompass still wider fields of observation—but it still remains valid, even then, as a subtheory which holds true for its previously structured field of inquiry. Thus if, as the fourth order of inquiry, theory of unconscious experience should fail to withstand the accumulations of further evidence, it could not make further claim to scientific warrant for its statement and application. If, that is, it no longer proves fruitful—a possibility which is quite conceivable but most improbable— its fate in psychoanalysis is no different from that of any theory in any other structure of science. It is either supplemented with theory to explain the new evidence or replaced by another to integrate the new with the old. As stated in *U*, it is the best now available. In this theory, then, there are psychological processes and patterns which can be so observed, defined and transformed that they exhibit both conscious and unconscious dimensions. And in practice, processes and patterns of signifi- cance for psychoanalysis are understood to develop configura- tions according to the incidence of anxiety and counteranxiety such that their range of progressive and regressive movement can be directly observed in the immediate field of their inci- dence. As transferred and countertransferred into the experien- tial field of therapy, moreover, these processes and patterns be- come available for inquiry, together with those of resistance and counterresistance, so that their genuine and distorted character may eventually be derived from the systematic orders of transformation and explanation.

Confirmed over and over again by direct observation in the experiential field of therapy, a major support of this theory is the postulation of two distinct modes of experience—immediacy and reflection. It requires little clinical acumen and even less spec- and patterns of pathological, dream or drug states do not resemble ulative metapsychology to demonstrate that observable processes those of sane, waking and sober experience. The procedures by which these postulates of affective impulse and rational intelligence can be related to both direct and defined observation are very often complex and, for the individual case, in some respects even beyond duplication. No single model has yet been constructed, in any case, which adequately represents impulse and intelligence in all cases—the model of id therapy does well with chaotic and driving forces of impulse; the model of ego or interpersonal therapy does well with directive and integrative functions of intelligence; the model of shared experience thus far does well with the transactional field. It should prove possible, eventually, to expand this last model so that it includes the observational results of its two antecedent models across the whole range of personal psychology. The unfortunate absence of a single overall model of therapy, to date, is perhaps the main reason why operational definitions still play so crucial a role in the structure of inquiry. It is possible at present, however, to envision the construction of such an overall model. If, for example, instead of id impulse or ego defense, the content of transference were described as unitary processes and patterns possessing both these two and other postulated aspects of experience as well, the realization of psychoanalytic structure would not be so heavily dependent on second-order definitions because, at the same time, it would not be so exclusively devoted to the acceptance of one or another interpretive metapsychology. Transformations at the third order and explanations at the fourth order, on the other hand, would occupy a larger and far more significant place in psychoanalytic therapy. Explanatory theory in statement U may be taken, meanwhile, as outlining the boundaries of empirical and systematic analysis to which two clusters of operational definition in statements t, r, a and ca, cr, ct and three pairs of transformational postulates in statements G and F, S and D, I and R are both applicable and fruitful. Even before the interpretations of any metapsychology in statements $[M_n]$, it is proposed, the virtue of this structure of inquiry consists in its use as a methodological tool which cuts across the three clinical models so that, as a result, it becomes possible to envision an overall structure by which all three may give rise to experiences of psychoanalytic therapy.

(5) *Interpretation*

Prior to actual psychoanalytic inquiry, the distinction of conscious from unconscious experience need not be generalized, of course, to hold for all, some or even any gross experience. It is and has been so generalized in many past speculations of metapsychology, unfortunately, as to interpret the nature of gross experience which is not yet psychoanalyzed. These speculations may possibly stimulate some researchers to undertake inquiry into unexplored areas of gross experience and even goad others to make superficial parlor studies of persons unknown to them and experience untouched by them. But the results of such speculative efforts are not valuable as science, however, until they are also capable of empirical and systematic analysis under conditions of structured inquiry. It is at this fifth order of metapsychology, moreover, that all privilege of private preference and any speculation of arbitrary judgment may be freely exercised. As in other sciences, so in psychoanalysis: Any philosophies of nature and human nature which are held by its practitioners are logically distinguishable from the actual procedures by which they establish patterns of observation, definition, postulation and explanation that ground, specify, analyze and reconstruct the working validity of their structure of inquiry. There still is no way, yet, by which to fit all experiences of psychoanalytic therapy into one format, and this indefinite variety of psychoanalytic experiences has supported a prolific projection of highly speculative and often contradictory metapsychologies. For this practically countless number of individual experiences, however, it is possible to demarcate a structure of inquiry which is based on those intensively studied and which, therefore, earns for them the designation of psychoanalysis. This common clinical structure, above all, serves to relate one such experience to another, in so far as each experiential field of therapy is directed toward the goals of psychoanalysis. The attempt to organize psychoanalytic knowledge around four orders of observation, definition, transformation and explanation—and, thereby, encourage the individual practitioner to decide his preference in metapsychology—is no more than an attempt to demarcate a structure of inquiry so that, when properly realized, it becomes an instance which confirms the adequacy of the structure itself to generate still another among the indefinite variety of psychoanalytic experiences.

In this psychoanalytic structure, the serial orders tend to resemble a pyramid in which gross experience resembles its broad base and theory of unconscious experience, of course, its capstone. From first-order observation to fourth-order theory, there is no need for any rationale other than the construction of actual psychoanalytic inquiry, and nothing in logic or psychology militates against a reversal of this sequence—moving from fourth-order theory to first-order observation, instead, and describing the pyramid from, so to speak, top to bottom. Because observation is primary, however, and since systematic studies of this structure are few and far between, observation is put first in order to affirm the obvious value of such basic questions as the patient's active experience or his problems in learning and such answers which derive from structured inquiry in the field of therapy. Since publication of *Studies on Hysteria* over seventy years ago, the purpose of building a structure of psychoanalytic inquiry has remained consistent and clear—to construct a field of inquiry in which the fourth-order theory is best adapted to one person working therapeutically with another who is in distortion, disturbance or difficulty, so that unconscious processes and patterns are most capable of being fully experienced, explored and analyzed.

Turning to the fifth order, it is clearly in the light of this same purpose, as well, that all interpretive metapsychologies are to be understood. Each one, of course, is projected in the hope of uncovering various processes and patterns which are still unconscious but the projection, by now, of so many incompatible metapsychologies in so brief a history is rather disconcerting, however, to those who find psychoanalytic inquiry sound and scientific at the foundations of its structure. This large number of incompatible metapsychologies suggests, further, that universal agreement at the fifth order may not be reasonably expected on the basis of logic or empiricism. In any event, if only because no one has yet done more than to dream the metapsychology of a man living in outer space, the fifth order still remains wide open to new speculations about human nature. Firm and reliable though second-order definitions and third-order postulates now are, moreover, their coordinate applications have not yet been fully worked out in empirical inquiry. Often treated impressionistically in actual therapeutic experience and even more often applied as fragments of structured inquiry, these unfinished aspects also have not yet been systematically constructed for regular empirical procedure. The general outline of their structure is now firm, but further empirical work in accordance with postulates of immediacy and reflection will most likely best open psychoanalytic inquiry to the psychological problems of both learning and change and novelty and imagination in the making of new experience. Study of these problems is not restricted to the structure of psychoanalytic inquiry, clearly, or confined to the experience of psychoanalytic therapy. For they branch out to involve larger notions of need, goal, ideal and metaphor of experience—established metaphors such as machine and organism and, in recent metapsychology, the newer metaphors of stream and field. Without a single, uniform philosophy of nature and human nature which is widely accepted, however, these larger notions are not beyond dispute and cannot be integrated whole and undefined as empirical and systematic psychoanalysis. Pluralism, therefore, is the only viable position to take on metapsychologies at the fifth order. As long, finally, as the practice of psychoanalysis is in accord with the values of humanism, science and democracy—with those, especially, of individuality, truth and freedom—no more need be expected of patients considering the personal worth of psychoanalytic experience, in order to realize its structure of inquiry, than open but intelligent concern about the probabilities of psychological change.

There are in psychoanalysis metapsychological assumptions which have not thus far proved crucial to its clinical structure as inquiry or its clinical experience as therapy. They at times dominate research and affect the formulation of leading definitions and postulates, nevertheless, because psychoanalysts are accustomed to couching new clinical observations in philosophies of experience. Most major researchers evolve relatively unique networks of interpretations to go along with their advancements of therapeutic inquiry, while a few adopt the critical stance of refining and expanding—of, in short, reconstructing—one or another perspective already established at the fifth order of metapsychology. All these perspectives are based on themes and values which derive, of course, from both science and culture. But it is the mark of enduring psychoanalytic metapsychologies, in fact, to produce the widest criticism of personal experience, social behavior and cultural values without seriously contradicting the widest range of scientific knowledge.

Theory of personality, for example, represents an amalgam of results which are obtained in both clinical and experimental research as well as in perceptive analyses of society and culture, and it is to be found in all major psychoanalytic metapsychologies of the past. Thus far, psychoanalytic theory of personality development and disorder has ranged from the biological and sexual to the cultural and interpersonal as well as, more recently, to the religious and transcendental. In each perspective, however, the notion of personality serves as a methodological tool for delineating aspects of psychological patterning which arise from the philosophy of organism and environment, man and culture, experience and values. While Freud, for example, developed balanced theories—more or less biological—for the union of empirical observation and systematic transformation with judgments of philosophy and value, others like Adler, Jung or Rank were not as balanced in the substantive development of theirs. But these fifth-order theories, it is proposed, do not constitute the backbone of psychoanalysis. Clinical structure of first-order observation through fourth-order explanation does instead and, therefore, any contribution to psychoanalysis may now be evaluated in terms of its significance for the power of this structure to yield psychoanalytic experience. As metapsychology, then, philosophies of experience and theories of value are inevitably colored by each psychoanalyst's and each patient's experience of living and, as their interpretations of life, are invariably subject to individual differences which are often small but never meaningless.

History, it may be observed, supports this distinction of the first through the fourth from the fifth order of psychoanalytic structure. Over the years, the empirical and systematic orders have undergone clear and gradual enlargement and modification. From Breuer's original work in 1880 with the talking cure, it has developed through Freud's formulation of id therapy in his 1910-1915 papers and 1915-1917 *Introductory Lectures,* Reich's pioneering work on character analysis in 1932 and A. Freud's compendium of ego therapy in 1936, to Hartmann's 1939 expansion of ego psychology and Sullivan's novel procedures with schizophrenics and 1940 reformulations of theory; and though, by the middle forties, psychoanalysis developed into two wings along lines which separate classical and modified biological from cultural and social metapsychologies, since the late fifties major efforts have centered on ways to demarcate a psychoanalytic structure for a distinctive type of psychological inquiry into the personal range of shared experience.[13] This gradual enlargement and modification of psychoanalysis has been governed by a critical awareness of the utility of new observations which, in turn, have often stimulated further engagement in metapsychology—partly to assure the future of these new observations, of course, but mainly to honor the ingrown psychoanalytic custom of making large speculations about man's basic nature. In clinical fact, however, the original discoveries were usually sound and firm in their own terms and, to remain self-sustaining and self-corrective, only needed to be coordinated in a clearly ordered structure of psychoanalysis. But the distinction of the first through the fourth from the fifth order, on this account, becomes all the more significant. For neither empirically nor systematically, it is proposed, do established metapsychologies entail actual enlargements of the experiential field of therapy. Rather, it is the capability of psychoanalysts who can use similar operational definitions under similar conditions of inquiry and, in spite of deep differences in metapsychology, reproduce the pioneering observations which first inspired expansions of the field. Psychoanalysis may indeed be sound enough as clinical discipline, at present, to elaborate the structure of its inquiry so that it is productive and consistent yet distinct, as well, from the varieties of interpretive umbrellas which are spread out over varieties of therapeutic experience that result from its application. Such interpretive umbrellas are required, of course, as fifth-order perspectives on meta-psychology because every psychoanalyst and every patient need philosophy to live. At the fifth order of inquiry, individual and group differences among psychoanalysts and their patients pre-clude the detailed application of any single metapsychology to every single experience of psychoanalytic therapy. Pluralism in metapsychology is being suggested, therefore, in order to unlock the closed systems of fifth-order interpretation. It not only respects the best available knowledge of distortion, disturbance and difficulty; it also supports the reconstructing of empirical and systematic orders of inquiry and, in sum, is compatible with the traditions of humanism, science and democracy.

B.   SPECULATION

The habit of metapsychological speculation is firmly rooted in psychoanalytic thought. When this habit is considered in the light of the fact that it does not produce empirical or systematic constituents of therapeutic inquiry, the question of its meaning becomes all the more perplexing. It may be instructive, here, to take a brief look back at the serial ordering of psychoanalytic structure. Why, for example, does the psychoanalyst move his inquiry from direct observation to operational definition? And why does he then transform defined observations by means of general postulates? To put it simply: He can use newly trans-formed observations, together with those originally defined, to explain distortion, disturbance and difficulty by his theory of unconscious experience. After defining in this structure the operation of transference, for example, through observation of selected particulars of gross experience, he seeks postulate

transformations of these now defined observations for the express psychoanalytic purpose of demonstrating the persistence
of their unconscious processes and patterns. Now, the question
naturally arises, why formulate a fourth-order theory to explain the particulars of gross experience which are thus far
observed, defined and transformed? And the most direct answer is, because it is there to be formulated. This is a simple
statement of fact, perhaps too simple to accommodate the deeply
rooted habit of metapsychological speculation but, in any case,
just as valid and defensible as the traditional answers which
are used to justify the fact of this theory. It may be argued,
of course, that most psychoanalysts do not generally proceed
by this way of explicit definition and conscious postulation.
But even if this is true of them, it is hardly true of all psychoanalysts—a few may still proceed with careful attention to their
structure of inquiry. From the fact, moreover, that a majority
is indifferent to the structure and its empirical, systematic and
interpretive orders of inquiry, it cannot be argued that this
structure and these orders do not already exist—to be explored,
applied and reconstructed. Nor from the fact that this proposed structure guides but a small minority, furthermore, does
it follow in logic or empiricism that its application is any the
less feasible or fruitful.

The need to answer this question, why the theory of unconscious experience altogether? triggers the impulse to varieties
of metapsychology which are based on factors as varied as instinctual dialectics, struggle for power, collective unconscious,
pure will and so on, and whose common denominator it is to
produce a rationale for unconscious psychology by interpreting
its contents. The real problem of psychoanalysis today, however,
is no longer that of debating the relative merits of basic reasons
why certain but not other processes and patterns are uncon-

sciously experienced. It is no longer the problem, today, of relating empirical and systematic inquiry to the interpretive results of these speculative efforts. It is now necessary, instead, to draw a thin yet indelible line in psychoanalysis between psychology and metapsychology and, by this line, remain aware of the clear and inviolable differences between them. This approach is being set forth because, in the relations of psychology and values, pluralism above all other perspectives on metapsychology most closely reflects the values of humanism, science and democracy.

The distinction of the whole structure of inquiry from its perspectives on metapsychology may be understood, in psychoanalysis, to follow that of matters of fact from matters of belief. In the psychoanalytic study of individual or group psychology, the point where fact and belief intersect is itself, of course, a very complex subject of empirical inquiry. Whatever the results, however, intersections of fact and belief do not diffuse or transform the one into the other. Perspectives on metapsychology may be justified, obviously, in the ways that beliefs are generally justified—by appeal, persuasion, dialectics and even coercion—while this structure of psychoanalytic inquiry concerns a subject matter whose meaning and interpretation are partly composed of belief but whose processes and patterns are fully amenable to empirical and systematic inquiry. As long as uniformity of belief and conformity in action cannot be derived from a philosophy of man's basic nature, and as long as individuality and integrity of the human psyche remain values of live experience, the wish to gain acceptance for any one such philosophy in psychoanalytic therapy as against any other is, therefore, inevitably inspired by elements of whim, caprice, prejudice and sentimentality. And if the history of psychoanalytic metapsychology provides a clue, moreover, it is that men will probably continue to inhabit this common world of experience and inquiry and, at the same time, articulate radically different philosophies of that world.

Every science is limited by systematic measures which surround and restrict all empirically grounded generalizations about gross experience. Here, again, is the line between personal appeal and persuasion which seek assent and reliable knowledge and inquiry which are open to further reconstruction. It is drawn, of course, to coincide with the distinction of science from philosophy of science in the organization of psychoanalytic knowledge. It has already received indirect support from past, recurrent and perhaps inevitable differences in metapsychology which are still clear and present, today, in the references to schools, groups and movements and, when somewhat negative, even to sects, cults and priests of psychoanalysis. They also are clearly present in highly charged disputes over matters of belief in the fifth order, reflecting many well established differences in philosophies of experience and value. As matters of belief, however, they invariably subtend every experience of psychoanalytic therapy no less, yet no more than any other experience which involved that particular psychoanalyst with that particular patient. But they need have no internal effects on empirical and systematic inquiry and, as metapsychology, need no more be intruded than excluded. Simply and generically, they are in the field of psychoanalytic therapy, to be attended or ignored in the evolution of any particular shared experience in accordance with the commitments and individualities which its co-participants bring to it. No matter how thorough the study of these differences, clearly, it still leaves undone the study of the psychological processes and patterns bearing them, especially the unconscious dimensions of these and other processes and patterns.

Historically, psychoanalysis grew up supported by philosophies of turgid romanticism and burdened with the ceaseless reworking of opposites, polarities and dualities. It is still wrapped up in the drama of paradox and conflict, the strategies of attack and defense, the repressive and alienated mood. It pursues the processes and patterns of psychological distortion, disturbance and difficulty to their unconscious roots, and it does so on the assumption that its outcome is a variable whose achievement as patterning of behavior does not always require original experience and inquiry to make it an individual way of life. The values of turgid romanticism are already limited and rather boring, however, where they are not altogether mistaken and dangerous. To move along the stream of directly felt emotion without the directive and integrative factors of rational intelligence, in other words, is as difficult as reaching a selected point of a distant shore by freely floating beyond the breakers: It may sometimes be fun to float but, to reach that point, it is also good to know how to swim out there. To drop the metaphor: A perspective chosen from among the several philosophies at the fifth order and ranging from turgid romanticism to scientific humanism is still not, strictly speaking, a matter of psychological fact. Toward the end of the last century, psychoanalytic patients apparently knew what they were supposed to become but, so they believed, were failing to attain it. Patients consult psychoanalysts at present, it seems, because after becoming what they believe they should become, they then seek to regain a sense of what they still are capable, individually and genuinely, of becoming. They look out at a confusion of values to choose from, only to become more confused about what it means humanly to live and grow or, in a brief glance inward, encountering devastated self-esteem and even more confusion. They seem to suffer most in their interpersonal, cultural and social environment from deeply insecure relations to themselves—for which reason psychoanalysts are more frequently asking, "How do you respond to such-and-such situation?" in order to reach the intrapersonal environment. For patients keenly sense, today, that yesterday's fantasy may emerge as tomorrow's reality. If, in this circumstance, psychoanalysis is to continue being practiced with appropriate regard for its own empirical and systematic standards of intelligibility, it must distinguish its structure of inquiry from its several philosophies of life and, then, discover how particular metapsychologies differ from the particular fields of therapy in which they are or are not justified. No single perspective on metapsychology may be said to occupy the fifth order of this psychoanalytic structure: It is now clear that many do. And no single perspective may be said to govern its procedure: It is now clear that structure of inquiry does.

With social values and scientific technologies so much in flux, therefore, it becomes all the more important for the contemporary psychoanalytic patient to be free to disentangle the confusing from the reliable, the insecure from the stable, the remote from the immediate, in the study of his experience. For philosophy, today, is still confusing, insecure and remote— seeking bases for belief in firm psychological patterning of behavior which brings about reliable social consequences. But since, furthermore, psychoanalytic structure cannot support any necessary bonds or bridges between itself and any one philosophy of psychoanalytic experience, its fate as inquiry need no longer be inextricably intertwined with the metapsychology of its founders. This new age of atomic science, space and cybernetic technology, mass communication and expanding human rights has untold possibilities for the reconstruction of human experience and, while still seeking a well formulated philosophy, has clearly outgrown the movements of late nineteenth-century thought. If, in this yet unphilosophized age, patients would develop psychological awareness of basic directions of their lives, psychoanalysts must be able to apply a structure of inquiry which is open and receptive, at least, to the emergent philosophies of the present.

Chapter 4

Symbols of Representation

A NOTATIONAL SCHEME of psychoanalytic inquiry does not necessarily imply mechanical theories of mind, self or experience. While it is probable that some such scheme will eventually be made amenable to mechanical treatment by the new computers, all these results will remain bound by the conditions peculiar to such treatment. The conclusions which a machine can produce as being true of psychoanalytic experience, however, do not extend beyond the limits corresponding to observations and definitions, postulates and theory which already constitute empirical and systematic orders of psychoanalysis. This structure of inquiry in turn, of course, is not proved true by the ordered terms of the structure itself, and no machine can create the empirical and systematic relations which prove it or its results to be true, either. When the structure is applied to discrete and indefinitely extended observations of distorted, disturbed and difficult experience, its truth derives from its appropriate elaboration as this is now possible in the therapeutic field of psychoanalysis. A machine has to be programmed, it is clear, in terms of a notational scheme but, on its own, no machine can create a structure of inquiry, however, whose notational scheme symbolically represents actual subject matter. It is not even possible to know what in fact it would mean, at present, to assert that a machine could create any such structure of inquiry. For better or worse, psychoanalysts alone—those who work, that is, with perspectives, procedures and products of actual therapeutic inquiry—are capable of creating such a structure and who are prepared to accept responsibility for its adequacy. This they must do before attempting to produce its symbolic representation, and before submitting it to logical or computer analysis in order to research constituent probabilities which are implicit in any notational derivatives. Only human beings can produce a structure of inquiry of this sort, and only those who conduct inquiry in accordance with it can see it to be true. No matter how intricate the mechanisms or precise the calculations, no mechanical computer has yet programmed itself on the basis of a structure of inquiry which only it sees to be true—unless, at some future date, the unconscious patterning of scientific experience so changes that what it means to see a structure to be true is no longer identifiable either in current ways of thinking or by current terms of reference. But that future is nowhere near at hand. If it should ever arrive, however, the human terms of man's relation to the machine would also have to undergo very radical and unprecedented change, in order to sustain what now appear to be ineluctable differences between man and machine.

The following symbolic scheme is tentatively set forth as a matter of convenience, then, and for the sole purpose of representing the constituents of this psychoanalytic structure. Thus far, a scheme of symbolic representation, together with some of its provisional uses, can be outlined for the conduct of psychoanalytic inquiry. It lends itself to a number of applications and transformations, suggests various directions of clinical research, yet contains no more than a prolegomenon to possible future lines of symbolic representation. Such a scheme, it is clear, can be no better than the structure of inquiry which it represents, so that both are now being developed from an open and tentative point of view. This structure and this scheme may be no more than a beginning but, if it is possible to begin, there is nothing to be gained by avoidance and delay.

A. ORDERED INQUIRY

Table 1 is an overall scheme of representation for the structure of psychoanalytic inquiry. The operational bridge which relates t_n through ct_n to t through ct remains a matter of practical art. Construction of this bridge is most difficult to generalize in an orderly way, and its description is possible only in accordance with the personality of a particular psychoanalyst and his therapeutic approach to a particular patient. What he does in order to begin (1) and (2) in the experiential field of therapy, and how he goes about (3) and (4) to prepare, finally,

TABLE 1.—Symbols of Representation

Orders of Psychoanalytic Inquiry				
Empirical		Systematic		Interpretive
Observation (1)	Definition (2)	Postulation (3)	Theory (4)	Metapsychology (5)
transference t_n	transference t	genesis G	unconscious experience U	Freudian $[M_1]$
resistance r_n	resistance r	function F		Adlerian $[M_2]$
anxiety a_n	anxiety a	structure S		Jungian $[M_3]$
counter-anxiety ca_n	counter-anxiety ca	dynamism D		Rankian $[M_4]$.
counter-resistance cr_n	counter-resistance cr	immediacy I		. . .
counter-transference ct_n	counter-transference ct	reflection R		—— $[M_n]$

for (5), cannot be exactly derived from a set of inviolable procedural rules. Since commitments to metapsychology at present are conflicting both among psychoanalysts as a group and between them as individuals and their patients, a set of procedural rules for (1) and (2) cannot be laid down in advance for all fields of psychoanalytic inquiry. Each particular psychoanalyst develops a personal style of working by which he moves from (1) to (2), as he fits his work to the uniqueness of the particular patient before him. But no two psychoanalysts need work in precisely the same way—they cannot, indeed, if only because no two are exactly the same people with exactly the same experiences and metapsychologies. Even if, per impossible, they could all fit their work to a single mold, since no two patients are exactly alike in respect to their problems or their immediate experiences of therapy, it is most improbable that psychoanalysts could practice in a uniform way. This is no different in kind, of course, from the fact of radical individual differences among experimental scientists in the laboratory. But it functions differently, however, in psychoanalytic therapy. After constructing this bridge from (1) to (2), for example, psychoanalytic goals are realized in each therapeutic field through steady emphasis on the study of anxieties. Hence, the centrality of $a \cdot ca$,[1]* in relation to $t \cdot r \cdot cr \cdot ct$, for the experience of psychoanalytic therapy as distinct from experiences of other psychotherapies.

While the psychoanalyst structures his empirical and systematic inquiry, as psychoanalyst, by guiding his procedures in accordance with (2) through (4), both he and his patient participate in the observation of (1) and the interpretation at (5). It is the use of (2) through (4), in other words, that defines his special activities, as distinct from those of other psychotherapists, learning theorists, animal behaviorists, social and

---

* For Notes to this Chapter, see page 206.

cultural critics and commentators, and so on. Whether he can also finally provide a comprehensive theory of human experience for all cases at (5), however, may pose an interesting problem for the individual practitioner. But it does not pose a serious structural problem, yet, since the need for such theory does not arise from his empirical and systematic work and, conversely, his empirical and systematic work does not stem from such theory. Biological and social theories of personality, biological and social theories of character and universal or absolute theories of basic human nature, for example, all formally transcend the empirical and systematic orders of psychoanalytic structure. Even though construction of such theories may be partly based on actual psychoanalytic observation, their validity is also dependent on interpretive and speculative analyses at (5), which are quite different in form and intent from the terms and conditions of a psychological inquiry from (2) through (4). No matter which particular perspective on metapsychology a psychoanalyst adopts at (5), therefore, (2) through (4) define the structure of his inquiry which he shares with his fellow psychoanalysts. (1) through (5), on the other hand, include varieties of psychoanalytic experience deriving from psychoanalytic structure, and these varieties may be assorted in accordance with philosophies of experience and theories of value which he may properly assign to (5). From this, of course, it is also clear that (2) through (4) map the widest area of agreement among psychoanalysts, since these orders comprise all common definitions, postulates and theory of their structure of inquiry, while the special perspective any psychoanalyst adopts with any patient at (5) is a likely attempt to define specific needs, goals and ideals of gross experience at (1) which accompany psychological processes and patterns that he singles out for study in (2) through (4). But if, in his adopted perspective at (5), the values of humanism, science and democracy prevail, he may restrict himself—as far, of course, as possible—to applying (2) through (4) to the distorted, disturbed and difficult processes and patterns of (1), and then leave the metapsychological judgment of their experience and value—as far, again, as he possibly can—to his patient's determination, instead of turning this psychoanalytic experience into a specially interpreted instance of his own perspective at (5).

(1) *Observational Field*

With an eye toward simplicity of presentation, the definition of transference, for example, has thus far been symbolized as t. But t, like $r \cdot a \cdot ca \cdot cr \cdot ct$, is a central definition of psychoanalytic inquiry. It may now be instructive to see how this second-order definition is coordinated with the structured orders of inquiry, from (1) through (5) as outlined in Table 1, in order to illustrate how operational definitions relate to the theory of unconscious experience in accordance with a specific set of symbolic representations. All definitions may relate, of course, to this fourth-order theory by similar sets of symbolic representations, but it is being attempted with t, here, for two reasons. If, first, this definition can be satisfactorily worked out, then the others may be expected to yield similar results; and second, even though it is still the psychoanalytic definition whose manifestations are best known, its general statement is not yet free of controversy. As a central definition, moreover, together with ct, it may be said to provide the empirical parameters of structured inquiry.

When the patient undertakes to present difficulties in living whose resolution he hopes to achieve in psychoanalytic therapy, it becomes possible to begin (1) in order to institute the special structure of psychoanalytic inquiry. And it becomes necessary to secure observations of special psychological aspects of his difficulties such as statement

(A) t_n

which describes the existence of processes and their patterns—
feelings, thoughts, attitudes—which are definable as instances of
statement

(B) t

which asserts the observed operation of such processes and
patterns as satisfy the requirements of this definition. But since,
as observed, t_n does not represent isolated events, it may prove
necessary to continue at (1) with observations which can be
supported within the structured range of statement

(C) $t_n \cdot r_n \cdot a_n \cdot ca_n \cdot cr_n \cdot ct_n$

and which at (2) may be stated in

(D) $t \cdot r \cdot a \cdot ca \cdot cr \cdot ct$

but whenever psychological processes and patterns can be both
observed and defined across the entire range, the transactions of
psychoanalyst and patient are as fully engaged as it is possible
for them to become under the empirical conditions of psychoanalytic inquiry. In this set of symbolic relations, t becomes
fully explored as it goes through the whole range of (1) and
(2), and only as it finally exhausts ct. These symbolic relations
also suggest, of course, the temporal, continuous and cumulative dimensions of psychoanalytic experience. Since, in statements (C) and (D), t is structured for the orders of inquiry, it
is necessary to proceed not only to its empirical relations to
other first-order observations and second-order definitions in
accordance with the actualities of a particular therapeutic field,
but it is also necessary to proceed to its systematic relations to
third-order postulates of genesis and function, structure and
dynamism, immediacy and reflection—in accordance, again,
with the actualities of a particular therapeutic field—hence,
statement

(E) $t_n \cdot t \cdot G \cdot F \cdot S \cdot D \cdot I \cdot R$

in which any thorough analysis of defined observations of transference must be open to the various postulate transformations, even if they are not explicitly undertaken with all six. For the structured inquiry, any postulate can be invoked to guide transformation of t such that its explanation is governed by the theory of unconscious experience. Symbolically, each one may be separately represented as, for example, in statement

(F) $t_n \cdot t \cdot G \cdot U$

which asserts that, as direct observations of the patient's gross experience initiate the structure of psychoanalytic inquiry, as the operational definition of transference is applied to observed processes and patterns of distorted, disturbed and difficult experience, and as the postulate of genesis is introduced to guide the transformation of historical and developmental aspects of those defined observations of transference, then the fourth-order theory of unconscious experience may be invoked to explain discrepancies, for example, among motives and attitudes expressed and, in turn, their incongruities with motives and attitudes experienced. As unconscious processes and patterns of transference are explored, however, to fix the reasons for unconscious aspects of the experience, it is necessary to expand statement (F) to the fifth order, as in statement

(G) $t_n \cdot t \cdot G \cdot U \cdot [M_n]$

by which some aspects of interpretive metapsychology—philosophy of experience and theory of value—that patient and psychoanalyst hold individually or in common, again comes into awareness during therapeutic inquiry and, from this, the attempt can be made to reinterpret as well as reconstruct distortions, disturbances and difficulties of transference.

Recall, now, statement (D) which relates t to its coordinate second-order definitions, especially to ct, the other parameter of

empirical psychoanalytic inquiry. To indicate this, statement
(G) may be expanded as statement

(H) $$t_n \cdot ct_n \cdot t \cdot ct \cdot G \cdot U \cdot [M_n]$$

which symbolizes postulate of genesis, theory of unconscious
experience and pluralistic perspectives on metapsychology, as
these may be systematically applied to defined observations of
transference and countertransference in their empirical convergence during psychoanalytic therapy. And it asserts: Observations of transference and countertransference, when firmly so
defined, may be transformed from a genetic point of view so
that their unconscious processes and patterns can be interpreted
in accordance with the metapsychological views of both participants. Note, however, that the genetic postulate is being separately applied while, during actual inquiry, it may be applied
to empirical observations in conjunction with any or all other
postulates. For the full third-order treatment of transference
and countertransference, it is possible to expand statement (H)
to cover all postulate transformations, as in statement

(I) $$t_n \cdot ct_n \cdot t \cdot ct \cdot G \cdot F \cdot S \cdot D \cdot I \cdot R \cdot U \cdot [M_n]$$

so that, by now, the notion of transference no longer merely
defines a series of first-order observations. By this full postulational treatment, it develops into a full-fledged psychoanalysis
of transference and, depending on $[M_n]$, now belongs to one or
another established metapsychology—Freud's, Adler's, Jung's,
Rank's and so on. Again note, incidentally, that since $[M_n]$ is
open to diverse speculations about experience and values,
this symbolic representation of the psychoanalysis of transference in statement (I) accommodates any new perspectives on
metapsychology.

It is clear, however, that $t_n \cdot t$ relates to defined observations
other than $ct_n \cdot ct$, as in statements (C) and (D), so that a full
symbolization of empirical, systematic and interpretive orders
of psychoanalysis for the study of transference may be repre-

sented by combining statements (C) and (D) with (I), as in statement

(J) $t_n \cdot r_n \cdot a_n \cdot ca_n \cdot cr_n \cdot ct_n \cdot$
$t \cdot r \cdot a \cdot ca \cdot cr \cdot ct \cdot$
$G \cdot F \cdot S \cdot D \cdot I \cdot R \cdot$
$U \cdot$
$[M_n]$

which demarcates the five orders of inquiry, and which structures the most general psychoanalytic treatment of any observation of transference and countertransference, resistance and counterresistance, anxiety and counteranxiety. Table 2 depicts the operation of this structure of inquiry within the field of therapy. It suggests how distinctive qualities of the patient's experience of therapy derive from the distinctive character of the pychoanalyst's structure of inquiry. Also note, however, that each constituent of statement (J) acquires a coordinate use and meaning in terms of the structure as a whole. Just as t, for example, gains full sense and adequacy in terms of r to a through $[M_n]$ inclusively, so every other symbolized constituent attains its full sense and adequacy in the coordinate terms of the remainder of the structure. The articulation of any term in this structure, therefore, must at some point include reference to its coordinate terms throughout the five orders of inquiry. As a consequence, for example, no theory of anxiety suffices for the conduct of therapeutic inquiry unless it takes full account of all structured terms, cutting across observation, definition, transformation, explanation and interpretation. Observation and definition alone, however, provide empirical foundations for relating the psychoanalyst's to the patient's self-actions, inter-actions and transactions, and modifying them in accordance with the psychoanalytic significance of their various processes and patterns. Apart from this structure, moreover, no psychological process or pattern may be said to acquire any psychoanalytic significance at all. It is in this sense, of course, that constituents of statement (J) are considered the irreducible terms of psychoanalysis which its structure of inquiry posits for achievement of its experience of therapy. There still are no satisfactory extrapsychoanalytic yardsticks by which, furthermore, to measure their reliability with quantitative accuracy. Even though this scheme of symbolic representation of the structure has yet to be developed along quantitative lines, it

TABLE 2.—Field of Inquiry

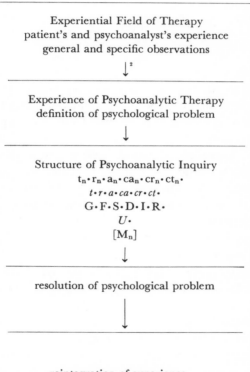

Experiential Field of Therapy
patient's and psychoanalyst's experience
general and specific observations

$\downarrow^2$

Experience of Psychoanalytic Therapy
definition of psychological problem

$\downarrow$

Structure of Psychoanalytic Inquiry
$t_n \cdot r_n \cdot a_n \cdot ca_n \cdot cr_n \cdot ct_n \cdot$
$t \cdot r \cdot a \cdot ca \cdot cr \cdot ct \cdot$
$G \cdot F \cdot S \cdot D \cdot I \cdot R \cdot$
$U \cdot$
$[M_n]$

$\downarrow$

resolution of psychological problem

$\downarrow$

reintegration of experience

should in fairness be said that it provides the most meaningful coverage now available for working out actual procedures and products of psychoanalytic therapy. Quantitative analysis is theoretically possible but, as in every other symbolic scheme, this type of analysis would yield nothing more than practical convenience which may be adopted where useful and ignored where useless. This theoretical possibility aside, however, inquiry does not begin without t, end without ct or have structure without $t \cdot ct$. It is difficult to add anything which better clarifies the methodological significance of transference and countertransference, if that significance is not already clear.

(2) *Defined Observation*

In thoroughgoing inquiry, all gross experience which is observed as t_n to ct_n may be expected simply to emerge, even though it is not possible for the psychoanalyst to apply t to ct through the whole range, all at the same time and each with the same intensity. As inquiry progresses, definitions may all be successively applied, but the logical possibility of dealing with all six in a single effort is still beyond the range of practical probability. Serially and, in some special instances, conjunctively, these definitions nonetheless prepare observations of gross experience for systematic inquiry. In Table 3, rows 1 and 6 represent parameters of the empirical side of the inquiry. Column F is most interesting, however, since $t > r > a > ca > cr > ct^3$ represents transactive phases in which both participants are fully engaged. Although t and ct represent empirical parameters, the terms of the psychoanalyst's participation, $ca \cdot cr \cdot ct$, do not ordinarily become operationally significant until a, either as $t \cdot a$ or as $r \cdot a$, moves front and center in therapeutic inquiry to dominate a special phase of the work—which, incidentally, is not easy to predict in any particular temporal sequence but, nonetheless, is required for any structure to be-

TABLE 3.—Schedule of Definition

	A	B	C	D	E	F	G	H	I	J	K
1	*t*	*t*	*t*	*t*	*t*	*t*					
2		*r*	*r*	*r*	*r*	*r*	*r*				
3			*a*	*a*	*a*	*a*	*a*	*a*			
4				*ca*	*ca*	*ca*	*ca*	*ca*	*ca*		
5					*cr*	*cr*	*cr*	*cr*	*cr*	*cr*	
6						*ct*	*ct*	*ct*	*ct*	*ct*	*ct*

come psychoanalytic. Note, also, that *t* does not suffice, once inquiry begins, as a lone and isolated definition. To defend, armor or secure transferred attitudes against their probable reconstruction in accordance with the actualities of the therapeutic field, a patient confronts his psychoanalyst with resistance, and both participants then have to undertake an intensive study of *r*. The point, now, of exploring *t·r* is to apply postulate transformations and explanatory theory such that relations of *t·r* to *a*, properly interpreted in $[M_n]$, may so free the patient from anxiety that it enables him to choose whether he would or not reconstruct his transferred attitudes in accordance with the actualities of the therapeutic field.

Recall column F, however, which contains the crucial descriptive notation for a structure of inquiry whose central feature, setting it apart from other psychotherapeutic inquiries, is its emphasis on the relation of *a* and *ca*. Also reflected in this column about the order of observation, however, is the fact that *cr* ordinarily emerges before *ct* is to be seriously treated. This does not simply result from the classical injunction against violating the psychoanalyst's incognito because, in point of fact, even when this injunction is not strictly obeyed, analysis of *ct* does not ordinarily precede the patient's encounter with *cr*. But since, however, *t·ct* demarcate the operational boundaries of psychoanalytic inquiry, may it not be assumed that *ct* is potentially definable from the beginning of inquiry? And why, then, does the effort to define it usually take place, when it does, after the definition of *cr*? Why, in short, do *cr·ct* fall into this order? For empirical answers to these questions, it is necessary only to consider *a* and—especially after it becomes fully operant—its impact which tends to obscure the effects of *ct* and so limit the patient's awareness that he even ignores those of its manifestations which otherwise would be immediately apparent to him as probable reasons for *a*. In other words, he cannot form a clear and useful perception of his psychoanalyst's significant processes and patterns, about which he already is resistive and to which his own anxieties blind him. Nor, obviously, can he make a genuine judgment of his psychoanalyst's basic beliefs and values and, as a consequence, make the far more important judgment of whether his own anxieties are genuine or distorted—in response to something genuine or distorted, that is, about either his psychoanalyst, himself or both. From a systematic point of view, however, *ct* clearly takes logical precedence over *cr* and *ca* because it is both a necessary and a sufficient condition of its functional correlates. Without the countertransference of feelings, thoughts and attitudes—no matter if their experience, on inquiry, is later called conscious, unconscious or mixed—there would be nothing about which to develop and manifest counter-resistances and counteranxieties. There would be no point, indeed, to suffering and undergoing them.

Table 3 may be read: if *t* in row 1, then *r* in row 2; if *r*, then *a* in row 3; if a, then *ca* in row 4; if *ca*, then *cr* in row 5; if *cr*, then *ct* in row 6—where, again, rows 1 and 6 are the empirical parameters of observation and definition, and where the syste-

matic transformations and explanations have yet to be carried
out, in order to expand and analyze the originally defined observations of gross experience. It may also be read as distinct
but integrated steps, beginning with column

A t

which is a condition for column

B $t > r$

which is a condition for column

C $t \cdot r > a$

which is a condition for column

D $t \cdot r \cdot a > ca$

which is a condition for column

E $t \cdot r \cdot a \cdot ca > cr$

which is a condition for column

F $t \cdot r \cdot a \cdot ca \cdot cr > ct$

and so on to column

K ct

where, again, in the well rounded experience of psychoanalytic
therapy, t is studied first and ct last, while the empirical and
systematic study of $a \cdot ca$ is central to that therapy which is structured as psychoanalytic inquiry. The fact that a particular inquiry is not carried through to the full realization of its structure, however, does not make it any the less meaningful or useful in the patient's life. A negative instance does not invalidate
an empirical proposition but only modifies its degree of probability—which means, by the same taken, that failure of this
structure in any one case does not undo its empirical founda-

tion and systematic integration in cases where it succeeds, to the extent that it does produce distinctively psychoanalytic experience.

Column C illustrates some relations among definitions which represent certain regularities of observation. From statements $t > r$ and $t \cdot r > a$, of course, it is clearly possible to derive statement $t \cdot r \cdot a$. When these notations are modified to suit the psychoanalyst's terms of participation, they yield the parallel statement $ca \cdot cr \cdot ct$. Together, both statements contain the second-order definitions of psychoanalytic inquiry. In accordance with the dominant definition in a particular context, it is proposed, any phase of the work ought thus to be capable of symbolic representation. Thus, too, the empirical significance of t may be stated as a function of $r \cdot a$ or $a \cdot r$, r may be stated as a function of $t \cdot a$ or $a \cdot t$, and a may be stated as a function of $t \cdot r$ or $r \cdot t$. A parallel series of statements can be derived, of course, from $ca \cdot cr \cdot ct$. But $a \cdot ca$—or the contexts, that is, in which a and ca intersect in various ways—represents the operational core of empirical inquiry. The point of r and cr among second-order definitions, therefore, is to obtain a closely detailed study of a and ca which identifies the special character of psychoanalysis as both inquiry and therapy. As $t \cdot r \cdot a$ emerges, moreover, and as this set of definitions is transformed by postulates and explained by theory, to discover elements of $[M_n]$ contained and carried by t, $r \cdot a$ at some points provides psychological contexts for the analysis of these discovered elements, but they do not involve questions of individual value for either participant until $t \cdot r \cdot a \cdot [M_n]$ is worked through in relation to $ca \cdot cr \cdot ct \cdot [M_n]$.

Table 3 represents, at best, an ideal schedule of defined observation. In reality, however, because of myriad possible manifestations of observable processes and patterns to be defined, when the causes of termination can be located in columns A through K, they take effect at any point after column A, de-

pending on conscious and unconscious experience of both participants. Any study of the conditions of termination has to
use some such device as Table 3, in one form or another, if
outlines which depict them are to be arranged in an orderly
way. The progression from columns A through K suggests a
general pattern which represents the empirical range of exploration in the particular case. When the patient makes an
immediate judgment of value during the first sessions and, on
the basis of it, decides to discontinue the work, this therapeutic
inquiry may go no further than column A. As column A becomes a condition for column B, any particular inquiry may
terminate because resistances become too strong, continue to
column C and then terminate in the face of powerful anxieties,
terminate at column D when counteranxieties overpower constructive attitudes toward the inquiry, at column E when coun-
terresistances unduly circumscribe the range of explorable
anxieties or signal the emergence of impassible disagreements
over philosophy and value, or at column F where the transactions of psychoanalysis are fully engaged and where transference and countertransference finally touch, intertwine and
even interlock. If the inquiry does get beyond column F, it
may continue to column G because transference no longer
presents any disruptive issues, to column H because the distinction of anxieties from counteranxieties can be clearly drawn,
and to column I through column K because the psychoanalyst's
individual experience becomes as clear to the patient as, in
column A, the patient's originally was to the psychoanalyst.
At this point, of course, a clear basis for termination may now
be symbolically represented within the possibilities and limits
of psychoanalytic inquiry.

It is also possible, now, to suggest how second-order definitions may be symbolically elaborated. Of special clinical interest, moreover, is this basic terminology for structure of in-

quiry under whatever metapsychology. Although many disagreements may still persist about the choice of some definitions
or postulates—and, perhaps, about the modification and exclusion of others—a very wide consensus undoubtedly supports
this choice of unconscious experience as the theory which
governs the demarcation of its structure of inquiry. In no sense
is this programmatic structure being developed, of course, as a
final and closed system. Its definitions, $t \cdot r \cdot a \cdot ca \cdot cr \cdot ct$, are being
set forth only tentatively; they appear in similar observational
patterns, involve similar postulate transformations and theoretical explanations and, at the fifth order, remain open to varieties of interpretation and speculation which extend beyond
the empirical and systematic orders. Thus, for example, the
symbolic statement

$$t_n \cdot t \cdot G \cdot F \cdot S \cdot D \cdot I \cdot R \cdot U \cdot [M_n]$$

which fully represents the place of transference in psychoanalytic structure asserts:

> (1) particular observations of gross experience can be made
> so that (2) they fall under the definition of transference, so
> that (3) they can be transformed by the postulates of genesis
> and function, structure and dynamism, immediacy and re-
> flection, so that (4) as both defined and transformed, they
> can be explained by the theory of unconscious experience
> and, finally, so that (5) in accordance with preferred per-
> spectives on metapsychology, they can be interpreted by
> philosophies of experience and value.

While the other five operational definitions also fit this format,
and while they may be readily stated in this proposed scheme
of symbolic representation, a serial listing of them would now
serve no special purpose. What this format reveals, most strik-
ingly, is that psychoanalytic treatment of any operational definition does not stop at first and second orders of inquiry. To be

systematic, it is clear, such treatment must continue through the third, fourth and, to satisfy requirements of personal experience, finally through the fifth, as well, in accordance with fundamental and believed interpretation of life. Instead, therefore, of a similarly lengthy statement about each, refer directly to Table 4.

TABLE 4.—Structure of Defined Observation

Operational Definition	Orders of Inquiry
transference	$t_n \cdot t \cdot G \cdot F \cdot S \cdot D \cdot I \cdot R \cdot U \cdot [M_n]$
resistance	$r_n \cdot r \cdot G \cdot F \cdot S \cdot D \cdot I \cdot R \cdot U \cdot [M_n]$
anxiety	$a_n \cdot a \cdot G \cdot F \cdot S \cdot D \cdot I \cdot R \cdot U \cdot [M_n]$
counteranxiety	$ca_n \cdot ca \cdot G \cdot F \cdot S \cdot D \cdot I \cdot R \cdot U \cdot [M_n]$
counterresistance	$cr_n \cdot cr \cdot G \cdot F \cdot S \cdot D \cdot I \cdot R \cdot U \cdot [M_n]$
countertransference	$ct_n \cdot ct \cdot G \cdot F \cdot S \cdot D \cdot I \cdot R \cdot U \cdot [M_n]$

(3) *Postulate Transformation*

Second-order definitions of the patient's and psychoanalyst's participation naturally fall into clusters of *t·r·a* and *ca·cr·ct*. These may be arranged, for example, as in statement

(A)

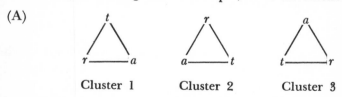

Cluster 1   Cluster 2   Cluster 3

each with its own alternative which is realized by transposing its two lower terms, so that *t·r·a* of Cluster 1, for example, becomes *t·a·r* and so on. But their special merit, however, is that they illustrate the coordinate relations of definitions. Since it may also be assumed, furthermore, that *t·r·a* are ordinarily observed to occur in one cluster or another, it may also be assumed, following the pattern of Cluster 1, that when a patient may be represented as first manifesting transference, he may later be expected to become resistive and anxious, though not necessarily in that order; or that, following the pattern of Cluster 2, when he may be represented as first manifesting resistance, he may later be expected to become anxious and transferential, though not necessarily in that order; and that, following the pattern of Cluster 3, when he may be represented as first manifesting anxiety, he may later be expected to become transferential and resistive, though not necessarily in that order. These patterns also hold, of course, for the various clusters which can be derived about the psychoanalyst's participation from $ca \cdot cr \cdot ct$.

In order to depict ongoing sequences of inquiry, another useful adaptation of these clusters of definition is to chain them to postulates which guide their transformation. If, for example, a patient may be represented as first manifesting transference and later becoming resistive and anxious, as in statement

(B) $\qquad\qquad\qquad t(r \cdot a)$

and if, then, the psychoanalyst attempts to transform it by the postulate of genesis, as represented in statement

(C) $\qquad\qquad\qquad t(r \cdot a) \cdot G$

and since the postulate of genesis is usually paired with that of function, this enlarged transformation may be symbolized by enlarging statement (C) into statement

(D) $\qquad\qquad\qquad t(r \cdot a) \cdot G \cdot F.$

Now, by depicting statements (B) through (D) as one unit, the transaction in which a patient may be represented as first manifesting transference, and whose psychoanalyst then attempts to transform it by the postulate of genesis, may be represented as a whole by statement

(E)

and in a similar way, it is possible to represent the transaction in which a patient who first manifests resistance, and whose psychoanalyst then attempts to transform it by, for example, the postulates of structure and dynamism, as in statement

(F)

or represent the transaction in which a patient who first manifests anxiety, and whose psychoanalyst then attempts to transform it by, for example, the postulates of immediacy and reflection, as in statement

(G)

it being understood, of course, that the two lower terms of each cluster may be transposed, and that a particular psychoanalyst may incline toward the use of different pairs of postulates in the case of each cluster of definitions. By combining statements (E), (F) and (G), however, it is possible to depict sequences of psychoanalytic inquiry by clusters of definition and chains of postulate, as in statement

(H)

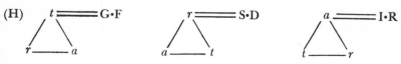

where G·F may also be chained to $t(a·r)$, S·D to $r(t·a)$ and I·D to $a(r·t)$. In each case, of course, choice of paired postulates for transforming the dominant definition of a cluster also depends on the specific cluster of definitions which, at that time, characterizes the psychoanalyst's participation. Some definable observation of the psychoanalyst's own experience may begin to occupy the center of inquiry, it is clear, even before the patient responds with resistance to the attempted genetic-functional transformation of transference. Suppose, for example, a patient cooperates in the genetic-functional exploration of transference and, meanwhile, begins to discover information about himself which, for some then unaccountable reason, makes the psychoanalyst observably counteranxious, to which the psychoanalyst may respond by shutting off the stimulus and attempting another postulate transformation, to which the patient may respond in resistance because he is then unable to deal directly with any dimensions of transference other than genesis and function, to which the psychoanalyst may respond in countertransference because of his own accustomed response to resistance which emerges after he already has been counteranxious, and the patient may then respond to countertransference in anxiety, which the psychoanalyst may find necessary to counter-resist by attempting the postulate of immediacy— but in order to unravel such chained clusters of psychoanalytic inquiry as represented in statement

(I)

it becomes necessary to be able to return, if still possible, to the first chain in this sequence, that of G·F, to learn what processes and patterns in the patient's history or function make his psychoanalyst counteranxious. If this is no longer possible, however, and with no success at postulate transformation of counteranxiety, the therapeutic alternatives may be considered so limited as to require repetition of the sequence into which they originally fall. At these points, of course, therapeutic inquiry becomes interlocked, but this interlocking does not frequently occur at so many points in such a full pattern. Not that it cannot but, simply, that it usually does not—either because the psychoanalyst in the face of his own counteranxiety begins to terminate the inquiry or continues to ignore particular genetic processes and patterns which first evoke his counteranxiety, and pursues the inquiry in other directions; or because the patient simply resists any further serious inquiry because of unexplored and perhaps idiosyncratic reactions to the counteranxiety of authorities or authoritarians, and begins to terminate before a fully interlocked pattern can develop. This may be unfortunate for both participants, however, since this is where psychoanalytic inquiry takes place in depth. In the particular therapeutic field, patient and psychoanalyst are more frequently in open or tacit agreement about focusing for intensive inquiry on one or another cluster of definitions and its pair of postulates—agreement being based largely on still unconscious processes and patterns which, for all practical purposes, are beyond the limits of that particular therapeutic field. These purposes range from a patient's conscious decision to select a chained cluster which appears to be most beneficial for resolving his problem, a psychoanalyst's conscious decision to ignore certain chained clusters for clear and shared or private and indeterminate reasons, a tacit recognition by one participant of the other's unconscious limitations, to the unrecognized and unconscious limitations of both. But when the field of inquiry is open and where the psychoanalytic structure is intently applied, even the unconscious dimensions of these purposes may later become appropriate subjects of inquiry and therapy.

Crucial phases of most psychoanalyses, however, can usually be fitted to these clusters and chains, and when therapeutic movement is reasonably good, it is far easier to realize how this fit is being made. Seasoned psychoanalysts tend to pursue a rather well organized approach, relying on one or another postulate transformation of one or another operational definition, and they usually accept patients in accordance with this special character of their approach. It may be suggested, as speculation, that those who work best with historical and developmental transformations usually select transferential personalities for therapeutic inquiry; those who work best with structural and dynamic transformations usually select the resistive personalities; and those who work best with immediate and reflective transformations usually select the anxious personalities. The bulk of a particular psychoanalysis may finally consist, therefore, in the resolution of one such cluster—depending, obviously, on the psychoanalyst's no less than the patient's contributions to therapeutic inquiry. Following the ordered structure, however, psychoanalysis cannot be limited to any one definition or postulate. Recall statement (E), for example, which depicts a chained cluster of transformed definitions of a patient in transference. If he remains for the full exploration, he may also be expected to encounter and work through resistance and anxiety, as well as some aspects of counteranxiety, counterresistance, countertransference. Or recall statement (F) which depicts a chained cluster of transformed definitions of a patient in resistance. If he remains for the full exploration, he may also be expected to encounter and work through transference and anxiety, as well as some aspects of counteranxiety, counterresistance, countertransference. Or, finally, recall statement (G) which depicts a chained cluster of transformed definitions of a patient in anxiety. If he remains for the full exploration, he may also be expected to encounter and work through transference and resistance, as well as some aspects of counteranxiety, counterresistance, countertransference. Table 5 is a synopsis of the results of transforming any defined observation in accordance with established postulates,

TABLE 5.—Transformation of Defined Observation

Postulate and Theory	Symbolic Representation	Transformation	
		Empirical	Systematic
genesis and unconscious experience	$x_n \cdot x \cdot G \cdot U^*$	forgotten and repressed	unconscious history and development
function and unconscious experience	$x_n \cdot x \cdot F \cdot U$	parataxic and disjunctive	unconscious communication and relatedness
structure and unconscious experience	$x_n \cdot x \cdot S \cdot U$	underdeveloped and unintegrated	unconscious pattern and organization
dynamism and unconscious experience	$x_n \cdot x \cdot D \cdot U$	unrealized and unfulfilled	unconscious striving and goals
immediacy and unconscious experience	$x_n \cdot x \cdot I \cdot U$	distorted and incongruous	unconscious feeling and impulse
reflection and unconscious experience	$x_n \cdot x \cdot R \cdot U$	irrational and illogical	unconscious observation and inference

* Depending on which defined observation is being transformed, $t_n \cdot t$, $r_n \cdot r$, $a_n \cdot a$, $ca_n \cdot ca$, $cr_n \cdot cr$ or $ct_n \cdot ct$ may be substituted for $x_n \cdot x$. Note, also, that $[M_n]$ is omitted, since each psychoanalyst introduces his particular metapsychology and, if he is a pluralist, openly welcomes each patient's introduction of his.

and explaining the results in accordance with established theory.

In applying these results, every psychoanalyst has to develop an abiding regard for the individuality of each particular patient and for some initially unknown and unconscious factors which are specific to his particular therapeutic experience. Most important among such factors, from the standpoint of psychoanalytic outcome, are desire to change and capability of changing. Desire to change is always hard to measure but, according to experimental psychometrists, this is not impossible. Capability of changing, however, need have but a frequency of one during extended psychoanalytic study of three to five years, and that study may nonetheless be considered successful. Although some constituent processes of this capability can be analyzed, only the rare patient remains long enough after it occurs to analyze it even partially—which makes sense in our culture, at least, because success is rarely held close to the light. Even if a patient did make the effort, moreover, it is still difficult to cross that thin line between the private and the most private, and bring back systematically useful knowledge. For since he makes this crossing only with the aid of metaphor and analogy by way of fantasy, dream and unconscious experience, when he returns with his new capability, he changes it for integrated communication in new public forms which no longer remain recognizable even to himself as that original most private experience. Only general characteristics which are uniformly observed and applied, however, constitute a structure that can be recorded and arranged in this notational scheme.

Still another way to represent the interlock of transference and countertransference may be derived from clusters of definition. Chains of postulate, however, are not being included since, formally, their possible symbolizations become practically infinite. The fact that all interlocks observed during psychoanalytic inquiry may not fit this formal map is no criticism of it, because such a map mainly attempts to highlight significant relations among definitions, represent a logical order into which they unfold, and alert practicing psychoanalysts to therapeutic possibilities other than those actually encountered with particular patients or regularly encountered with many patients. For if this formal map entails the therapeutic possibilities implicit in all actual psychoanalytic therapies, its symbolic representation also entails the interlock of transference and countertransference.

If, for example, the patient begins in transference, the cluster of definition depicting his experience may be depicted as statement

(J)

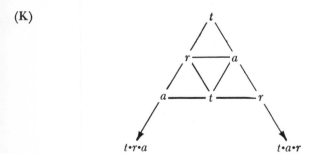

and, as therapeutic inquiry progresses, he may later be expected to become resistive and anxious, which may be depicted as statement

(K)

it being understood, of course, that even before the patient spontaneously begins to resist, the psychoanalyst's effort at postu-

late transformation of transference may hasten the full emergence of resistance. No matter, however, which pair of postulates is introduced—G·F, S·D or I·R—if the patient first
transfers, then resists and then becomes anxious, and if therapeutic inquiry proceeds to encompass the psychoanalyst's response, the field may now be depicted as statement

(L)

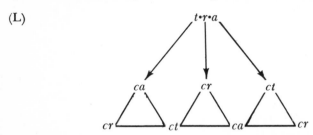

depending on the psychoanalyst's response to his patient's
cluster of definition. Assuming, now, that he first becomes
counteranxious, then counterresists and then countertransfers,
the resulting interlock of transference and countertransference
may be depicted as statement

(M)

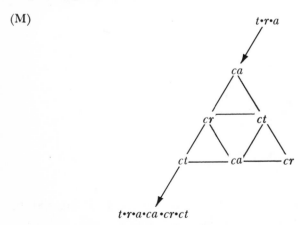

so that the full range of defined observations in psychoanalytic inquiry are operant. In this turn of events, statements (J), (K), (L) and (M) may be combined as statement

(N)

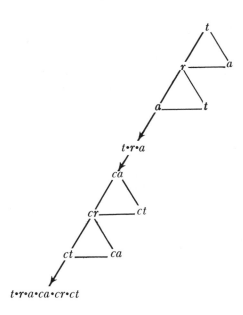

In this formal representation of transference interlocking with countertransference, only cluster $t(r \cdot a)$ is being fully symbolized. There are two other basic clusters defining the patient's participation, $r(a \cdot t)$ and $a(t \cdot r)$, two other basic clusters defining the psychoanalyst's participation, $cr(ct \cdot ca)$ and $ct(ca \cdot cr)$, three pairs of postulate, $G \cdot F$, $S \cdot D$ and $I \cdot R$, explanatory theory, U, and metapsychologies $[M_n]$, applying to all six basic clusters, which may appear at earlier or later points of the inquiry. It is therefore conceivable that an interlock may occur earlier in the therapeutic relationship, and that the development of cluster $t(r{\cdot}a)$, above, simply outlines one way to depict the interlock of transference and countertransference.

(4) *Explanatory Theory*

The structure of any particular psychoanalytic therapy generally follows from the individual patient's distortions, disturbances and difficulties, and from his presentation of them. It would be just as true to say the same about the psychoanalyst's metapsychology, personality and procedure: These, of course, are also individual and variable. But in any therapeutic inquiry, the emphasis throughout remains focused on the patient and his problems. It is his desire to change, above all, that makes the experience of psychoanalytic therapy, for whatever knowledge psychoanalysis could contribute to such change would be to no avail, obviously, without a patient's express desire for it. When the patient attempts to present his disturbances, even before deciding to undertake psychoanalytic therapy, he may predominantly relate in transference, resistance or anxiety. This does not mean that, if one predominates, the other two are therefore outside the clinical picture and do not later become relevant, but only that the one is at that point the best observable process or pattern for therapeutic inquiry. If he is predominantly in transference, this may be symbolically represented in statement

(A) $t(r{\cdot}a)$

just as his predominant resistance may be symbolically represented in statement

(B) $r(a{\cdot}t)$

or his predominant anxiety may be symbolically represented in statement

(C) $a(t\text{·}r)$

and in their variants, where the symbols in parentheses become operant in reverse order as the structure of psychoanalytic inquiry is accomplished.[4] Although, without the patient, there obviously is no experiential field of therapy, observations of his operant personality do not, by themselves, constitute the psychoanalytic character of that therapeutic field. As, therefore, processes and patterns of, say, statement (A) begin to unfold, their representation may quickly expand into statement

(D) $t(r\text{·}a)ca(cr\text{·}ct)$

or into statements

(E) $t(r\text{·}a)cr(ct\text{·}ca)$

and

(F) $t(r\text{·}a)ct(ca\text{·}cr)$

and into their variants because, necessarily, the psychoanalyst responds in some definable way to his patient. In statements (D) to (F), the first and fourth symbols represent dominantly describable processes or patterns in transaction, while those in parentheses may later become dominant as the psychoanalytic structure continues to be accomplished. Note, again, that these definitions are being symbolically represented with t as their point of reference; they may just as easily be symbolized with r or a as their point of reference. Hence, the second order of a series of sessions can be symbolized by such clusters of definition to represent specific phases of the work, encompassing the experience of both participants and, at a glance, revealing the central thread of that series.

In ordered inquiry, however, processes and patterns of statements (D to (F) then require postulational treatment—transformation, that is, in accordance with postulates of genesis and function, structure and dynamism, immediacy and reflection. Within a particular psychoanalyst's limits of capability and awareness, he chooses postulates on the basis of such factors as the particular patient's rhythm and flow of communication, requirements of extratherapeutic life, and real or imagined crises in experience. When, in accordance with such factors, he decides to attempt historical exploration, again using transference as his point of reference, the structured transformations may be symbolically represented in statement

(G) $t(r{\cdot}a)G(F{\cdot}S{\cdot}D{\cdot}I{\cdot}R)$

or if he then decides to attempt the postulate transformation of function, still using transference as the point of reference, it may be symbolically represented in statement

(H) $t(r{\cdot}a)F(G{\cdot}S{\cdot}D{\cdot}I{\cdot}R)$

and so on through S and D, I and R. Although it is ordinarily quite difficult to transform a defined observation by the simultaneous use of two postulates, it is frequently the case that a defined observation may be transformed in sequence by a pair of postulates. This does not necessarily take place in the same or consecutive sessions, because the genetic transformation in statement (G) need not necessarily be accompanied by the functional transformation in statement (H) or any other transformations of the remaining four postulates, until other sorts of defined observations have meanwhile been explored—those of anxiety transformed by the postulate of immediacy, for example, or those of resistance by the postulate of structure. Regardless of the interval between sessions, however, and no matter the extent to which other defined observations have yet to be explored—resistance, anxiety and counteranxiety, counterresistance, countertransference—when a genetic transformation of transference has been accomplished and its functional transformation is under way, the structure of inquiry may at this point be symbolically represented in statement

(I) $t(r \cdot a)G \cdot F(S \cdot D \cdot I \cdot R)$

and, of course, as unconscious aspects of transference are also revealed by these transformations, explanation of the repressed, distorted and unrealized aspects of the original observations may then be symbolically represented in statement

(J) $t(r \cdot a)G \cdot F(S \cdot D \cdot I \cdot R)U$

while full transformation and explanation of transference may be symbolically represented in statement

(K) $t(r \cdot a)G \cdot F \cdot S \cdot D \cdot I \cdot R \cdot U$

although full transformation is rarely carried through to full explanation in the individual case, partly because empirical exploration of transference is usually fragmentary and partly because an observation rarely reappears in identical form, with identical content, under identical conditions. A more limited transformation, as exemplified in statement

(L) $t(r \cdot a)G(F \cdot S \cdot D \cdot I \cdot R)U$

or in statement

(M) $t(r \cdot a)F(G \cdot S \cdot D \cdot I \cdot R)U$

usually suffices, however, for maintaining continuity of the inquiry. If statement (K) were now combined with statement (D), however, in which transference was originally taken as the starting point, the full range of empirical and systematic inquiry may be symbolically represented in statement

(N) $t(r \cdot a)ca(cr \cdot ct)G \cdot F \cdot S \cdot D \cdot I \cdot R \cdot U$

or by removing the parentheses from the psychoanalyst's cluster to suggest that his responses to transference are randomly counterresistance and countertransference as well as counteranxiety, statement (N) becomes statement

(O) $t(r \cdot a \cdot ca \cdot cr \cdot ct) G \cdot F \cdot S \cdot D \cdot I \cdot R \cdot U$

while, to obtain full empirical and systematic statement which includes the first order of observation, statement (O) may be simply expanded into statement

(P) $t_n(r_n \cdot a_n \cdot ca_n \cdot cr_n \cdot ct_n) t(r \cdot a \cdot ca \cdot cr \cdot ct) G \cdot F \cdot S \cdot D \cdot I \cdot R \cdot U$

and in retrospect, now, statements (A) to (O) may also be simply expanded in the same way to include symbolic representations of first-order observation. Any therapy of transference, because it has empirical and systematic constituents of psychoanalytic structure, can be represented by the terms and context of statement (P). And with interpretive and speculative metapsychology, finally, statement (P) may be expanded to represent the outside limits and possibilities of this structure, as symbolized in statement

(Q) $t_n(r_n \cdot a_n \cdot ca_n \cdot cr_n \cdot ct_n) t(r \cdot a \cdot ca \cdot cr \cdot ct) G \cdot F \cdot S \cdot D \cdot I \cdot R \cdot U \cdot [M_n]$.

Since the phenomenology of actual therapy indefinitely extends in every direction of its five orders of inquiry, it cannot be fitted to any a priori molds. Linkages, therefore, among clusters of definition, chains of transformation, lines of explanation and perspectives of interpretation and speculation cannot be laid down a priori, either. In actual phenomenology, it is soon clear, structure of inquiry is not simply found; it has to be built, instead, out of certain observations which are specially selected from the experiential field of therapy because, in fact, they do furnish definable processes and patterns for various postulate transformations, which it is appropriate to explain by the theory of unconscious experience and interpret by perspectives on metapsychology. Even from session to session, this notational scheme is therefore useful for symbolizing a structure which may be loosely construed as a grammar of psycho-analysis. It is not proposed, of course, that all phases of all psychoanalytic experiences have to fit this symbolized structure but, rather, that this structure encompasses crucial phases of all experiences of therapy in so far as they are products of psychoanalytic inquiry.

Symbolic representation, however, need be neither pragmatic in an operational sense nor practical in an immediate way. On a session-to-session basis, terms and relations of psychoanalytic structure may as well be written out longhand and, it is clear, be equally valuable for psychoanalytic therapy. Yet, from session to session, it does at a glance provide an adequate sense of what is happening, how it has come about, and what still remains to be done—from, that is, a psychoanalytic point of view. If, for example, the psychoanalyst notes that he seems continually to work with defined observations of transference and, in so doing, fails to attend to those of resistance and anxiety or, from the other side, seems continually to engage his patient when his patient observes countertransference and, in so doing, fails to attend to counteranxiety and counterresistance, he could refer back to his symbolic representations of the developing inquiry to see which defined observations are being emphasized, slighted, deflected or omitted. The same holds true, of course, for the various postulate transformations—which he seems to favor or bypass with which patient—and, also, for both the frequency and precision with which he can apply explanatory theory to certain observed, defined and transformed processes and patterns; he may even discover where, when and how his interpretive metapsychology tends to function in his therapeutic inquiry. By using some such symbols of representation as these to depict the developing inquiry, he may easily summarize the main work of each session, moreover, so that in some cases he may later be enabled by direct inspection to read the movement of any particular stretch of work which is actually being accomplished.

(5) *Interpretive Metapsychology*

This scheme of symbolic representation is being suggested only as a shorthand to depict the structure of psychoanalytic inquiry. As such, therefore, it is no more relevant to actual inquiry than the structure which it symbolizes. But it does reflect the crucial features of this structure, nonetheless, and it does demarcate psychoanalytic from other psychological inquires—experiments in psychopathology, projective testing and personality evaluations, for example, as well as the other psychotherapies—which also take place under the initial conditions of any experiential field of therapy. Its primary significance, thus far, resides in the plain fact that it can be done. For it illustrates the type of structure which is relevant to psychoanalytic inquiry and, at the same time, outlines the empirical and systematic basis of alternatives to absurdist and mystical metapsychologies of the recent past.

Any symbolic scheme will eventually require interdisciplinary development to supplement and refine its representations of psychoanalytic structure. Yet, the relation of this structure even to the structure of language, for example, involves many large and still unresolved problems. Even within this relatively gross scheme which represents its five orders of inquiry, first of all, the possible combinations among observations, definitions, transformations, explanations and both interpretations and speculations are practically infinite. These mathematical possibilities are not beyond comprehension as theory of inquiry but, at present, they are clearly beyond application as practice of therapy. There is, second, the problem of empirical and systematic significance in psychoanalytic inquiry which cannot be answered in terms of the structure of language in general or by the study of linguistics in particular. In an obvious sense, of course, the study of language is a useful approach to the structure of any scientific inquiry, and since significant processes and patterns of all psychotherapeutic experience at some point are matters of language in communication, it is no less relevant to that of psychoanalytic inquiry. But one is not the other. And third, it is not practically possible to weight the significance of any communication while it is under way—when, especially, the psychoanalytic observer himself is in the middle of responding to his patient. Why, it may be asked, does he have to respond? Why not become, instead, a sort of mirror or tape recorder? No matter the posture he may be urged to adopt, however, it does not affect this problem of assessing his patient's emergent communication. Such questions about the psychoanalyst's response are not relevant, strictly speaking, because this difficulty is neither procedural nor operational but, in fact, substantive. While, that is, the patient so communicates as to suggest, for example, emergent processes or patterns of change, his psychoanalyst cannot symbolically represent a change which does not yet exist to be observed, even though it may later be said to result from all prior observations, definitions, transformations, explanations and both interpretations and speculations converging at that particular point in the experience. No psychoanalyst can symbolize what he does not structure, and though he may observe, define and so on communications of the change in process, these provide but weak and unreliable clues to what is now happening—clues which, if symbolized, would probably be no better than empathic speculations of the seasoned practitioner. There is no getting around this fact: The emergence of new experience exists for inquiry only in so far as it is communicated, and its product can be observed only after it comes into existence, so the psychoanalyst often has to direct his unstructured inquiry along

that thin line at which the uncommunicated and unverbaliz-
able meet the communicable and verbalized.

Since the structure of language is itself a scheme of symbolic
representation, psycholinguistic theory can provide the psychoanalyst with only limited tools. This structure and this theory
both concern the verbalizable in particular and not the communicable in general. Nor, of course, do they explicitly concern psychological change or the psychoanalytic direction of it.
A patient's distortions in perception, disturbances in awareness
or difficulties in living, for example, are not ordinarily treated
as such in psychoanalytic inquiry but as symptoms of other
problems. In this way, the theory of unconscious experience
governs the structure through its first four orders—a tack which
is not suggested by practical logic or psycholinguistic theory;
they would suggest the opposite, if anything, and therapeutic
procedure would then no longer be psychoanalytic. Although
psychoanalytic study does not always entail fundamental
changes in the patient's actual environment, symptoms ordinarily tend to disappear as the disorders of which they are
symptomatic are adequately treated. Beyond this, finally, are
factors in every psychoanalysis which cannot be observed, defined, transformed, explained or interpreted until the patient
actually makes them known in some palpable way. Yet, these
factors may also become structured in inquiry as he gains the
sense of self direct enough to present new information about
himself and when, of course, he already has the freedom to use
it. This thin line at which the private meets the public in his
psychology, then, may eventually become intelligible within
its generative field of therapy. Only a radical empiricism is
illuminating here, however, because the personal qualities of
each patient are in some immutable sense uniquely his own
and do not identically recur in the experience of others. For
there are some experiences of a patient's life which only he
need feel or know.

Structure of language may be said to provide the conditions for rather than the conditions of psychoanalytic inquiry. Although not separable in theory or fact, these two sets of conditions are easily distinguished from one another and, because of this, are treated as belonging to distinct disciplines—in the same sense, clearly, that it is possible to study properties of a flower without necessarily studying properties of the plant from which it is cut, or know a vintage wine without going back to the place of its origin and studying the soil, sun, water and vines during the year the grapes were grown. Structure of language and structure of experience do not, in short, coincide. Psycholinguistics may perhaps include all linguistic theory but, from the standpoint of psychoanalytic inquiry, it hardly includes all psychology. Recall, for example, individual and qualitative aspects of experience which may grow and change from one stage of personal development to another while language remains fairly constant, or language repertoire which may grow and change from one stage of social and cultural development to another while psychic structure remains fairly constant. Consider, as well, that it is possible to have experiences which cannot be readily expressed in the language available, or master the grammar of a natural language without mastering the order of natural experience. The great grammarian may, indeed, be greatly insane. The view, furthermore, that categories of language determine psychological categories may well be an instance of the reductive fallacy: Is perception, for example, solely a function of language? does perception, to exist, have to be represented in language? or is language the only avenue to the study of perception? to the study of communication? even to the study of verbal behavior?—and these questions also suggest the point of a firm distinction between psycholinguistics and psychoanalysis.

Since language is a scheme of symbolic representation, any effort at a symbolic scheme for the structure of psychoanalytic inquiry is itself a symbolic representation of a symbolic representation. To serve the purposes of psychoanalytic structure, words have to be turned into other words and terms have to be turned into other terms. The study of psychology is not to be confused, however, with that of language behavior—or, for that matter, with that of social behavior or ethical values. The proper study of psychoanalytic psychology is, to put it as tautology, the study of psychoanalytic psychology.

B.   QUANTITATIVE ANALYSIS

A symbolic representation of psychoanalytic inquiry draws a map of psychoanalytic knowledge, relating orders of inquiry or levels of analysis but keeping them clear and distinct from one another. A map, however, is not a tour. It does not replace actual experience of the journey, it only identifies what route to take for a desired destination. No two trips along the same mapped route are ever identical in every detail, and no one resembles any other, obviously, along a different route. To drop the analogy: In psychoanalysis, structure of inquiry is distinguished from experience of therapy, and interpenetration of this structure with this experience is to be achieved in the field of therapy through the psychoanalyst's procedure and the patient's response to it. A symbolic scheme of this structure attempts merely to pinpoint relations to one another of (1) observation, (2) definition, (3) transformation, (4) explanation and (5) both interpretation and speculation. These five orders are being presented from a hierarchical point of view—from a view, that is, in which they point to their origins in the study of the patient's problems and their developments through the psychoanalyst's various empirical, systematic and interpretive operations. This mode of presentation is used to reflect structural orders of inquiry which may be realized in psychoanalytic therapy. It differs from the logical mode in which, for this study, (4) would precede (2) and (3) as the explanatory theory of psychoanalysis, and in which (2) would also precede (1) as psychoanalytic definitions for selecting from the patient's gross experience those communicated problems whose aspects of transference, resistance, anxiety a psychoanalyst can most confidently study because, at the present stage of developing knowledge, he knows the most about them. And it also differs, of course, from the interpretive mode in which (5) would precede (4), (3) and (2), and in which those aspects of (1) which support the psychoanalyst's or the patient's preferred perspective at (5) would first be selected for inquiry.

This symbolic scheme of representation does not provide, however, for a system of mathematical psychoanalysis in which quantitative manipulation of its symbolic terms yields direct observation of empirically controlled variables. Even if this were possible, furthermore, such a quantitative analysis need not prove useful since, indeed, no matter how rational or precise the mathematics of this psychoanalytic inquiry, its very neat results may be directly contravened by a patient's irrational assertions of will—it being assumed, for the moment, that his psychoanalyst's mathematics reflects perfectly even assertions of a rational will. Beyond this, finally, are the pervasive difficulties with quantitative methods for the study of novel experiences while these are emerging as a result of psychoanalytic inquiry. Unpredictable as to time and place of emergence, and unobservable as long as they remain just possible or potential, they still are the best leads available to the patient for reconstructing his distorted self. Although not yet relevant to the structure of inquiry, these emergent possibilities and potentialities nonetheless provide a patient with new leads to liberating experience in therapy. But they do not readily submit to quantitative analysis—they have to stand up, obviously, before they can be counted—and because they are novel, one communication of them has greater therapeutic significance than a thousand communications of established and recurrent patterns of distortion, disturbance and difficulty. This is not to imply that quantitative methods have no place in psychoanalytic research, but only to underline practical difficulties which obstruct efforts to quantify significant processes and patterns of psychoanalytic experience in their occurrence during actual inquiry.

About the quantitative study of psychoanalytic structure, then, two separate questions may be raised. First, can orders (2) through (4) be so treated mathematically that new relations among observable processes and patterns help to transform unconscious into conscious experience at order (1)? Given the necessary collaboration of practicing psychoanalysts and creative researchers, the eventual answer to this question, probably, is yes. And second, since psychoanalytic inquiry is always a matter of personal mastery for each psychoanalyst, does it not also become a matter of his particular application of it to each therapeutic field, as well, to meet the personal requirements of each particular patient? This second question suggests far greater difficulites which obstruct the regular use of quantitative methods. Now since the bridge spanning empirical orders (1) and (2) and systematic orders (3) and (4) always has elements of the interpretive order (5)—elements of philosophy and value which, as a rule, both psychoanalyst and patient contribute— the answer here, without doubt, is also yes. Quantitative methods have thus far floundered because they cannot be applied to each radically individual experience of therapy, they have thus far failed because they are not consistently applied to the distinctively psychoanalytic regularities of these individual experiences. Before quantitative methods become useful, in any case, there must be a structure of inquiry which clearly outlines orders or levels of analysis that constitute the regularities of psychoanalytic as distinct from other psychological fields of inquiry and therapy.

Chapter 5

Awareness and Responsibility

FREEDOM AND DETERMINISM, at the present time, are critical metaphors of all psychological therapy. This order of interpretive metaphors is, of course, as necessary to the materials of psychoanalysis as its empirical and systematic orders of inquiry. Even though they are metaphors of metapsychology, however, they are nonetheless necessary to the clinical study of human experience—from the instinct theories of classical Freudism all the way, obviously, to the Christian love of daseinanalysis. To put the difference briefly: Freedom supports and is supported by activity psychology and self-expansion philosophies of experience in which men are drawn to satisfy needs, secure goals and fulfill ideals. Determinism, on the other hand, supports and is supported by mirror psychology and energy-reduction philosophies of experience in which men are driven by needs, goals and ideals that press for satisfaction, security and fulfillment. Of the two, freedom is the superior guiding principle of psychoanalytic metapsychology, if only because it is far better aligned with the central values of humanism, science and democracy. It is possible, of course, to defend the values of authoritarianism in culture, absolutism in science and totalitarianism in society yet, at the same time, also uphold empirical and systematic requirements of psychoanalysis. In one respect, it is clear, these requirements are the same for all sciences: Personal and social values of their practitioners are to be distinguished from both the reliability of empirical procedures and the validity of systematic results. It is therefore appro-

priate, first, to review the outline of psychoanalytic structure
which distinguishes these empirical and systematic requirements from such interpretive metaphors as freedom and determinism and, second, to suggest certain of their relationships
which indicate where, in the actual experience of therapy, a
psychoanalyst's values end and his patient's values begin.

Recall the introduction to psychoanalytic structure in Chapter 2. This structure of inquiry is made up of (1) observations,
(2) definitions, (3) postulates, (4) theory and (5) metapsychology.[1]* As such, it is that branch of psychology which is designed to clarify the operation in personal experience of unconscious processes and patterns. Its central observations yield
two sets of definition—transference, resistance, anxiety to describe the patient and counteranxiety, counterresistance, countertransference to describe the psychoanalyst. These two sets of
defined observation, in whatever sequence and combination
they occur, may be transformed in accordance with the following postulates: genesis and function, structure and dynamism,
immediacy and reflection. Postulate transformations, then,
make possible still further observations which may be used to
explain problematic aspects of the original ones by the theory of
unconscious experience. All unconscious experience now re-
turned to awareness, however, depends for its interpretation on
the interpreter's—psychoanalyst's or patient's—philosophy of
experience and theory of value which, as distinct from empirical
and systematic psychology, is literally metapsychology. Since the
classical instinct theorists, various leading researchers have set
forth many different and even contradictory metapsychologies
as speculative interpretations of human experience—real and
distorted, whole and disturbed, at ease or in difficulty—those,
for example, of struggle for power, collective unconscious, pure

---

* For Notes to this Chapter, see page 206.

will and so on. In spite of these differences, the psychoanalyst's efforts at empirical and systematic inquiry derive, however, from a unified structure which also governs similar efforts of his colleagues. First, he makes observations of gross experience. Second, he introduces operational definitions which specify certain psychological processes and patterns that are observed in the therapeutic field. Third, he adopts postulates or points of view which transform these defined observations. Fourth, he applies to these now transformed observations the theory of unconscious experience which explains psychological problems that were originally defined at the second order. And fifth, he proposes one or several metapsychologies by which to interpret them as part of a general philosophy of life. No matter which he happens to believe and, in any case, to use—this being the point, essentially, about awareness and responsibility in psychoanalysis—his patient is free to adopt the perspective which suits his own existence.

Through this sketch of the ordered structure of psychoanalysis, it is now possible to draw a far clearer distinction of problems of awareness from problems of responsibility. Problems of awareness are studied in the empirical orders of (1) and (2) and the systematic orders of (3) and (4), while problems of responsibility belong to the interpretive order of (5). Through this sketch, furthermore, it is possible to draw this distinction across psychoanalytic structure so that studies of awareness are in the first four orders and studies of responsibility are in the fifth and, in this way, to support the parallel distinction of psychology from metapsychology.

These distinctions, of course, do not replace established models of psychoanalytic therapy. Instead, they strengthen its foundations, enlarge its scope and sharpen its focus by putting the psychoanalyst to work with his patient in a common field of therapy and by arranging a workable division of their empirical, systematic and interpretive labors. If they really do work together in a common field of therapy, however, and if one may be observed and defined just as appropriately in counteranxiety, counterresistance, countertransference as the other is observed and defined in transference, resistance, anxiety, then there is no doubt that the psychoanalyst is psychologically present. From this it follows, clearly, that his psychology ought to be open to study by and with his patient. But if this is true, it is also true that the patient is metapsychologically present. And does it not also follow, just as clearly, that his metapsychology ought to be as open to study by and with his psychoanalyst? Not unlike his patient, a psychoanalyst ought to stand in full measure behind both what he is in psychology and what he believes in metapsychology. To do so, however, he cannot but be prepared to receive psychological definition by his patient and to accept metapsychological difference from his patient. No single metapsychology, so far known, can be arbitrarily adapted to all patients, for differences in metapsychology inevitably arise in accordance with the individualities of each particular therapeutic experience. And responsibility is, actually, a question of metapsychology. To discover the boundaries at which his personal responsibility ends and his patient's begins, every psychoanalyst has to learn to fathom the depth and range of his own experience of every patient. For freedom to experience—to strive, to feel, to think, to relate—is most directly evident to its possessor in the actual fields of relatedness and communication in which it occurs.

What takes place during therapeutic inquiry is, in fact, the main source of observation which yields the problems of the inquiry. It is also the main source of conviction which derives from firm probabilities of responsible change. But no psychoanalyst attempts inquiry into all experienced problems of his patient's psychology. Nor can he, in any case, take personal responsibility for all his patient's actions in or around the experiential field of therapy. He is not his patient's parent, teacher, mentor or guide but, to put it simply and plainly, he is nothing other than that which his name denotes—one who does psychological analysis. Whatever else he does beyond psychological analysis of unconscious experience, he does in response to special and peculiar demands of his personal metapsychology. As psychological analyst, he is best prepared by both institute and clinical training, however, to participate in the study of those of his patient's psychological problems which appear in relation to himself—which makes it all the more important for him to have, at the very least, a secure sense of his own self in all his therapeutic inquiries. Now just as the psychoanalyst is not his patient's parent, obviously, the patient is not his psychoanalyst's child either. Nor is he student, disciple or in search of a moral guide but, to put it simply and plainly again, he is nothing other than that which his name denotes—one who suffers psychological problems. As psychoanalytic patient, therefore, he needs intensive psychological study of his distorted, disturbed and difficult experience, and he may reasonably expect changes toward clarification and improvement in so far as his distortions, disturbances and difficulties derive from the unconscious processes and patterns of his psychology.

To close with a comment on values in psychoanalysis: No matter how they are philosophically defined—as idealist or materialist, realist or pragmatic, absurdist or mystic—it is not possible for anyone to succeed at either practicing or undergoing psychoanalysis without genuine belief in such general values as individuality, truth and freedom. There are, of course, the middle-range values which are no less real and considerable. A patient may choose a psychoanalyst, for example, who happens to prefer symphonic music or cool jazz to rock and roll, French impressionism or abstract expressionism to pop or op art, or realistic films of wasteland and bedroom or western films of sex and violence to underground movies. But since these middle-range values of daily preference are far more variable than general values of overall significance, perhaps there is more room to differ about the former than about the latter without, however, seriously disrupting psychoanalytic inquiry. Where, in fact, a psychoanalyst tends to choose his patients on the basis of values in the middle range, and without genuine regard for general values, it is safe to expect that his intensive therapy will produce interlockings of transference and countertransference, resistance and counterresistance, anxiety and counteranxiety, or other combinations of these processes and patterns of shared experience.

On the relation of awareness and responsibility in psychoanalysis, then, while the psychoanalyst works as well and thoroughly as he can toward transformation of unconscious into conscious experience, it is the patient who has to answer all questions, finally, concerning his own responsibility. Awareness is psychology, responsibility is metapsychology, and their union as responsible awareness or aware responsibility is, in each case, a personal achievement to which each participant can guide only himself. Development of awareness need not be conceived as mystical illumination, religious conversion or unconditioned event which comes from out of the blue. A difficult and uncommon achievement, it may be conceived, rather, as made up of novel but strictly historical events that develop out of actual fields of relatedness and communication in which psychoanalyst and patient co-participate, communicate and collaborate. No psychoanalyst attempts to do it for his patient— he can no more do it for his patient than his patient can do it for him. To this end, he introduces a division of labor between, roughly, inquiry and therapy so that while participating to the full extent of his active powers of psychological inquiry, he may leave judgments of value to the final determination of his patient. And no matter how he then treats his patient, as one result of this division of labor, a patient treats himself therapeutically. This, of course, is an ideal statement of the distinction of inquiry from therapy, for it is not possible to experience psychoanalytic therapy in the absence of the psychoanalyst's structure of inquiry. The practical point of this division of labor, however, is to give the psychoanalyst responsibility for his structure of inquiry and to give the patient responsibility for his experience of therapy. With inquiry as psychology and with therapy as both psychology and metapsychology, what the psychoanalyst offers his patient in the way of firm psychological knowledge is far more useful toward realizing such general values as individuality, truth and freedom than anything he could possibly offer in the way of active and responsible direction of his patient's life. And these general values are to be found, no doubt, in any serious metapsychology of psychoanalysis which is aligned with humanism, science and democracy.

Notes

PREFACE

[1] See B. Wolstein, *Freedom to Experience* (New York: Grune & Stratton, 1964), pages 11-31 and 230-252, and *Transference* (second edition; New York: Grune & Stratton, 1964), pages 225-260.

[2] Below, page 157; refer, also, to pages 60-61 and page 101.

Chapter 1: EXPERIENCE OF THERAPY

[1] See, below, pages 24-37.

[2] On the psychoanalyst relating to his supervisor as his patient relates to him, see B. Wolstein, *Countertransference* (New York: Grune & Stratton, 1959), pages 64–67.

[3] See S. Freud, "Further Recommendations in the Technique of Psychoanalysis," *Collected Papers* (London: Hogarth, 1924), Volume 2, page 373.

[4] See J. Dewey and A. Bentley, *Knowing and the Known* (Boston: Beacon, 1949) on the notion of fact; also J. Dewey, *Logic* (New York: Holt, 1938) and E. Nagel, *The Structure of Science* (New York: Harcourt, Brace & World, 1961) on scientific theory; and I. Scheffler, *The Anatomy of Inquiry* (New York: Knopf, 1963) on fiction in scientific explanation.

[5] S. Freud, "Observations on 'Wild' Psychoanalysis," *Collected Papers* (London: Hogarth, 1924), Volume 2, pages 298–299.

[6] W. Reich, *Character Analysis* (New York: Orgone, 1945), page 3.

[7] Briefly reviewed in B. Wolstein, *Freedom to Experience* (New York: Grune & Stratton, 1964), Introduction.

[8] Traced in psychoanalysis to J. Breuer's contribution to his and S. Freud's *Studies on Hysteria* (New York: Basic Books, 1957) and, in philosophy, to Plato's *Republic*.

[9] Below, pages 63-75, see how third-order postulates and fourth-order theory interweave in systematic relation to a second-order definition.

[10] In B. Wolstein, *Transference* (second edition; New York: Grune & Stratton, 1964), Appendix A, this model is referred to as therapy of the total per-

sonality. Either model of shared experience or therapy of the total personality refers to the same transactional inquiry. The notion of shared experience more explicitly sets off special characteristics of this model, however, from those of both id and ego or interpersonal therapies.

[11] Below, pages 79-87, see further comments on structure of psychoanalytic inquiry, experience of psychoanalytic therapy, experiential field of therapy; especially Figure 1, page 84, and Figure 2, page 85.

Chapter 2: STRUCTURE OF INQUIRY I

[1] Compare, for example, W. Bion, *Elements of Pyschoanalysis* (New York: Basic Books, 1957) with D. Rapaport, *Structure of Psychoanalytic Theory* (New York: International Universities Press, 1960).

[2] For views on the problem of prediction which are compatible with this psychoanalytic structure, see B. Wolstein, *Transference* (second edition; New York: Grune & Stratton, 1964), pages 45–48, 226–229 and elsewhere.

[3] A. Whitehead and B. Russell, *Principia Mathematica* (Cambridge: Cambridge University, 1903), page 10.

[4] D. Hume, *An Enquiry Concerning Human Understanding* (Oxford: Clarendon, 1902), Section 4, pages 29–30.

[5] See Table 1, below, page 157.

[6] In this notation, x refers to the special observations of psychoanalysis—transference, resistance, anxiety and counteranxiety, counterresistance, countertransference—which are at this point interchangeable, and n to the practically infinite number of actual observations. But see Table 5, page 179, for other uses of this open type of notation.

[7] Developed in B. Wolstein, *Freedom to Experience* (New York: Grune & Stratton, 1964), pages 60-88.

[8] See, below, Chapter 4.

[9] Symbolic representation has definite advantages over discursive analysis, however, for depicting instances of multiple postulate transformations. See Table 5, below, page 179.

[10] See, for example, N. Chomsky, *Syntactic Structures* (The Hague: Mouton, 1957) and G. Miller *et al.*, *Plans and the Structure of Behavior* (New York: Holt, 1960), for one approach to these issues; also, below, pages 192–194.

[11] See Table 5, below, page 179.

Chapter 3: STRUCTURE OF INQUIRY II

[1] See Table 2, below, page 165.

[2] See examples of defined observations of the patient's and psychoanalyst's participation, below, pages 104–106.

[3] See Table 1, below, page 157.

[4] In *Principia Mathematica* (Cambridge: Cambridge University, 1903), page 11, A. Whitehead and B. Russell point out that definitions are neither true

nor false but that, without them, treatment of observations becomes so lengthy as to make a subject matter unmanageable. Also, see J. Dewey and A. Bentley, *Knowing and the Known* (Boston: Beacon, 1949), Chapter 7.

[5] In B. Wolstein, *Freedom to Experience* (New York: Grune & Stratton, 1964), especially Part II.

[6] This represents a defined observation such that statement t_n contains all observations to be made under statement t—which holds as well, of course, for statements r_n, a_n, ca_n, cr_n and ct_n in respect to statements r, a, ca, cr and ct.

[7] B. Wolstein, *Transference* (second edition; New York: Grune & Stratton, 1964), page 196.

[8] See below, pages 112–123.

[9] See below, pages 136–142.

[10] Described in B. Wolstein, *Countertransference* (New York: Grune & Stratton, 1959), pages 124–155.

[11] Compare S. Freud, *A General Introduction to Psychoanalysis* (Garden City: Garden City, 1943), pages 299-300.

[12] See Table 5, below, page 179.

[13] Elaborated in B. Wolstein, *Freedom to Experience* (New York: Grune & Stratton, 1964), especially Appendix.

Chapter 4: SYMBOLS OF REPRESENTATION

[1] • represents co-operation of symbols.

[2] ↓ or → represents sequences of inquiry.

[3] > represents conditioned relations of if–then.

[4] See, above, pages 173–174, for discussion of these variants.

Chapter 5: AWARENESS AND RESPONSIBILITY

[1] See Table 1, above, page 157, and Table 2, above, page 165.

Index